TABLE OF CONTENTS

INTRODUCTION

Water smoke cooking has become one of the most favorite and exciting additions to outdoor cooking. The simplicity of water smoking is one reason this cooking craze has spread. But the best reason is the juicy and delicious smoke flavor created by this extraordinary process.

Everyone takes pride in showing off their home smoked specialties. Why not? Every creation is a success! When family and friends sample those moist, mouth-watering, tender, smoked delicacies, they can hardly wait to create their own.

With very little attention and seasoning, you too can prepare terrific foods with a Cook'n Ca'jun water smoker. In addition to your favorite meats, you can cook fish and seafood, appetizers, vegetables, breads and even desserts. Using a water smoker of proven performance will give you the confidence to develop your own favorite recipes. It is so simple, even for the amateur. With proper equipment and guidance, there is no limit to how deliciously outstanding the results will be.

A versatile outdoor appliance, the Cook'n Ca'jun can be used to water smoke, steam, bake and grill. Easily converted, it is ready to grill those favorite steaks and burgers. As an extra, grill recipes have also been included.

This water smoker cookbook covers the smoking of basic foods, most enjoyed, with a few new suggestions. Although it is written with detailed instructions for the beginner, it provides the most experienced cook with exciting new ideas.

WATER SMOKING

The cooking principle used in today's modern water smokers is derived from a centuries old method of cooking with moist heat by placing the food over a pan of water to separate it from the direct heat of the fire. This method of water cooking was developed long ago in ancient Asia and was steadily improved upon until the 16th century, when it became a specialized art. Its use continued early into the 20th century until it began to disappear during the fading days of the Chinese Empire. However, here and there around the world, a few devotees continued to enjoy the benefits of this marvelous style of cooking. Some of those devotees were in the Texas and Louisiana area, where, by the late 1960's they had developed a variation in the original method of water cooking. They combined the cooking of food over water, for moist tenderness, with the use of wood smoke to add a tangy flavor. This cooking combination resulted in what has become well-known today as water smoking.

Water smoking is different from other methods of outdoor cooking, such as grilling or barbecuing over direct heat. Foods cook fast over direct heat, but require constant tending and turning to keep them from burning or overcooking. Water smoking, on the other hand, is a slow, moist cooking process with the added bonus of smoke flavoring. For example, small items of meat such as chops, sausages, or chicken pieces cook within two to three hours. Large items of meat such as turkeys and hams may take from five to eight hours to cook.

The water smoking process combines the cooking heat with moisture from the water pan and smoke from the flavoring wood. This mixture circulates up and around the meat inside the smoker and gives the meat a savory smoked flavor as it slowly cooks to perfection. During the cooking process, the meat is continuously basting in a mixture of the moisture from the water pan and some of its own juices. As this self-basting occurs, drippings from the meat fall back into the water pan where they provide further flavoring to the moist cooking process. The moisture in the heat prevents the drying out of meats as they cook and allows them to retain more of their natural juices. This reduces the amount of shrinkage that normally occurs from cooking. The moistness of the meat also allows more of the smoke flavor to be absorbed. The water smoking process works well with any type of meat, fowl or fish.

There are several advantages to water smoking. First is the delicious flavor. Any cook will be pleased and proud to serve their smoked specialties. The slow moist cooking process will enable you to serve less expensive cuts of meat that will please the most discriminating diner. An amateur cook can become a "gourmet chef" overnight.

Recipes can be simple seasonings or exotic marinades. Either way, the taste of water smoked meats is deliciously unforgettable. The second advantage is the ease of cooking. Once the smoker is made ready, and the food is prepared and placed, the rest is fuss-free. The food doesn't need tending or turning while it is cooking. You can relax and not worry about it until the time has come to take the food off. Third is the convenience and fun of cooking outdoors. The heat and mess stay out of the kitchen. The cook can enjoy parties or family gatherings without worrying about the food and cleanup. With these many advantages, it is no wonder water smoke cooking has become so popular.

Flavoring Wood

The smoke from flavoring wood is a prime ingredient in the water smoking process. The smoke is what gives the smoked foods their unique flavor. There are many types of flavoring woods. These include hickory, mesquite, apple, cherry, pecan, and orange woods. Any fruit or nut tree wood may be used for flavoring. Some of the more common of these are readily available in most areas of the country, while others can only be found in regions of the country where the trees are grown.

Hickory wood is one of the most popular flavoring woods. It is a good, all around wood to use because the hickory smoke flavor is good with all types of meats, fish, or fowl. It's a particular favorite with pork such as "Hickory Smoked Ribs" and "Hickory Smoked Hams".

Mesquite wood is a favorite in the southwest area of the country, and is fast becoming popular throughout the country. The smoke flavor of mesquite is very good with beef, especially smoked flank steak or smoked skirt steak.

Orange wood smoke is good to flavor poultry, pork, lamb and game birds.

Never use resinous woods such as pine or cedar, because they will produce an unpleasant taste.

Wood sticks, three to four inches long and 1-inch to 1½-inches thick, work best for water smoking. If sticks are not available, wood chunks comparable in size will work as well. Small wood chips or shavings do not work well for water smoking because they will burn too quickly and will not produce the desired smoking effect.

Unless the wood is green, which usually can only be obtained by cutting it from a live tree yourself, the wood should be soaked in water for at least an hour before using in the water smoker. If you use your water smoker often, it is a good idea, and a convenience, to keep a small supply of the wood soaking in a container. It will be ready for you to use at any time you want to do some water smoking.

The purpose for soaking the wood is to prevent it from burning up too quickly and to cause it to produce more smoke. For water smoking, it is best if the wood "smolders" slowly and continues to produce smoke for a longer period of time.

It does not require a lot of wood to obtain a good smoke flavor. Two or three sticks are usually the most you need to use for smoking even the largest items of meats. You will usually see a lot of smoke coming out of the top of the smoker during the first hour or so of operation. Although this will die down and you may not notice much smoke coming from the unit as the cooking continues, it does not necessarily mean that the wood has burned up and there is no more smoke. There probably is still some wood left and it has settled down to a very slow smolder. Upon closer examination, you will likely see some smoke still coming from the unit and smell the smoke aroma.

Know Your Water Smoker

Water smokers are designed to achieve the proper balance of moist slow cooking and smoking. We recommend that you become familiar with your water smoker and how to use it properly. The information that follows, and the illustration on the next page, describe the Cook'n Ca'jun water smoker. If you have another brand of water smoker, there may be some difference in the way it is made and how you use it. You should read the owner's manual that came with your unit to learn all about it.

The heat source for the water smoker is located at the bottom of the unit. This heat source may be charcoal briquettes, an electric element, or a gas burner. In Cook'n Ca'jun models, the heat source is housed inside of the base pan. The base pan keeps the heat inside the smoker for a more efficient operation.

The cylinder shaped smoker body sits directly on top of the base pan. The smoker body is equipped with heat and weather resistant handles on each side. The body can be lifted on and off the base pan to provide easy access for adding flavoring wood to the heat source. Also, on the charcoal models this provides easy access for starting the fire and for adding charcoal if more is needed during the cooking process. The smoker body is tall and cylindrical in shape so that it provides a "chimney" effect. It directs the moist heat and smoke up and around the foods being cooked.

The water pan is located inside of the smoker body, between the source of heat and the cooking grids that hold the food to be cooked. It is held in place by brackets inside the smoker. The purpose of the water pan is to separate the food from the direct heat and to serve as a source of moisture for the water smoking process. It is precisely located above the source of heat so the water will heat to a simmer during the cooking process. Moisture, in the form of steam, rises off the top of the heated water and mingles with the cooking heat and smoke as they circulate up and around the food. The water pan is larger for some models than others. The larger pans usually hold enough water to last throughout the entire cooking process, to accommodate foods that require long cooking times. It will usually be necessary to add water, after approximately four hours cooking time, to the models that have the smaller pan. Herbs, spices, onions, fruit and fruit juices, wines and marinades may be put in the water pan for extra cooking aroma. These will also add flavor variations to some types of meats.

Some models of water smokers are equipped with one cooking grid (referred to as single grill model) and others are equipped with two cooking grids (referred to as double grill model). In the single grill model, the cooking grid is located immediately above the water pan. In the double grill model, one cooking grid is located immediately above the water pan, and the second grid is located at the top of the smoker body. The cooking grids are made of chrome plated steel and are designed to hold up to 25 lbs. of food each.

A dome shaped lid is used to cover the top of the water smoker. The "dome shape" of the lid provides even cooking as it causes the heat and smoke, that rises to the top of the smoker, to recirculate around the food. Also, the dome provides additional space at the top of the smoker so that large items of meat can be cooked on the top grid. The lid fits loosely inside the top of the smoker body. Moisture that collects inside the lid will drain back down inside the smoker. This prevents messy runs and stains from appearing on the outside of the smoker. The spacing between the dome lid and side of the smoker provides ventilation for the unit to operate properly. The lid is also equipped with a heat and weather resistant handle.

Some models of the water smoker are equipped with a heat indicator. This may be located directly in the side of the dome lid or in the dome handle. The heat indicator allows you to monitor the cooking temperature inside the smoker. The food is cooking properly when the heat indicator is pointing anywhere in the "IDEAL" range. If the pointer drops to "COOL", you may need to add some charcoal briquettes to the fire in the charcoal models. If the pointer reaches "HOT", you may need to add more water to the water pan.

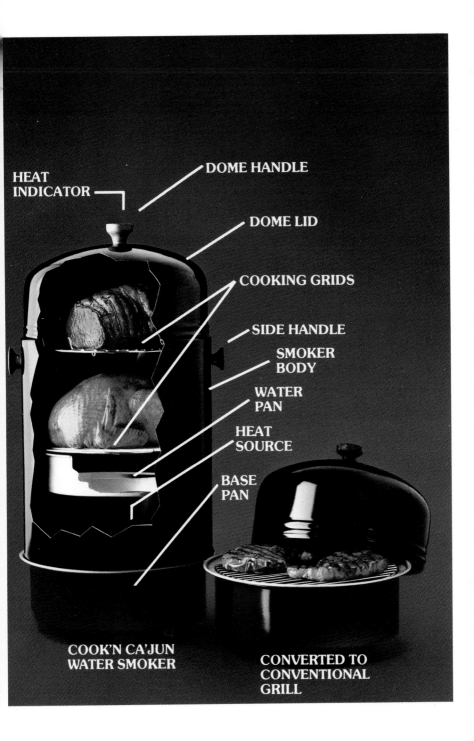

HEAT
INDICATOR

DOME HANDLE

DOME LID

COOKING GRIDS

SIDE HANDLE

SMOKER
BODY

WATER
PAN

HEAT
SOURCE

BASE
PAN

COOK'N CA'JUN
WATER SMOKER

CONVERTED TO
CONVENTIONAL
GRILL

The Cook'n Ca'jun water smoker is a versatile outdoor cooking unit. In addition to water smoking, it can also be used for dry smoking, barbecuing, baking and steaming. The unit can be quickly and easily converted from a water smoker into a conventional grill for broiling steaks, hamburgers or hotdogs over direct heat.

Tools for Water Smoke Cooking

Protective Mitts: Large, thick, heat-proof mitts are recommended when cooking outdoors. These will provide easy handling of hot equipment and hot food. They will prevent burns.

Long Handled Utensils: Select tongs, baster and turner with long handles for ease in moving food. These will also prevent you from touching hot surfaces.

Meat Thermometer: Using a meat thermometer gives you the most accurate measurement of doneness. Remember to insert the thermometer into the meaty part of the meat, with the point away from bone and fat.

Accessories for the Water Smoker

Rib Rack: The rib rack allows you to arrange ribs so smoke and moist heat vapors completely surround ribs to cook them evenly. The rib rack may also be used to bake potatoes and other vegetables. It may be used on either top or lower cooking grids on double smoker models. It is made of chrome-plated steel. Rib racks are available from your dealer or from Cook'n Ca'jun Products.

Step - Up - Grill: The step-up-grill adds an additional 182 square inches cooking area for smoking or barbecuing small pieces of meat, or for cooking vegetables. It may be attached to either top or lower cooking grid of double smoker. It is made of chrome-plated steel. Step-up-grills are available from your dealer or Cook'n Ca'jun Products.

Hickory Wood Sticks: Hickory wood is one of the most popular flavoring woods used for smoke cooking. They provide a tasty smoke flavor to any meat, fowl or seafood. Hickory wood sticks are available from your dealer or Cook'n Ca'jun Products.

Rib Rack

Step-up Grill

Using the Charcoal Cook'n Ca'jun

Always read the owner's manual for complete instructions on assembling and using your water smoker. Before starting, be prepared by carefully reading the recipe or cooking chart to determine advance preparation needed and the amount of cooking time required. The amount of food and the cooking time required will determine the amount of charcoal and water you will need. For best results follow these step by step instructions.

1. First, lift the smoker body off the charcoal pan and set aside.

2. Fill the charcoal fire pan with the amount of charcoal briquettes recommended. Briquettes should be arranged so they are nestled closely together in the bottom of the fire pan. This will allow briquettes to burn evenly and provide more consistent cooking temperatures from cookout to cookout. If briquettes are left in a heap, with large air passages between them, they will burn up more rapidly and give off hotter temperatures than are desirable for smoke cooking. The Cook'n Ca'jun charcoal pan will hold up to fifteen pounds of charcoal briquettes.

3. Sprinkle briquettes liberally with non-odor producing fire starter (½ to 1 cup) and wait three to five minutes before lighting. DO NOT USE gasoline, kerosene or alcohol to start charcoal fire. These fuels are unsafe for this purpose and may produce an unpleasant taste.

4. Light the charcoal with a match, being careful to keep hands and arms at a safe distance from the igniting flame. Allow coals to burn until they are without flame and beginning to gray (20 to 25 minutes).

5. Flavor producing wood sticks may now be added on top of the burning coals. Refer to the cooking chart or recipe for the amount to use. (Wood should always be pre-soaked in water.)

6. Replace smoker body on top of charcoal pan and remove the dome lid. Fill the water pan with the amount of water that is recommended in the cooking chart or recipe selected.

7. Put grid or grids on smoker. Arrange meat on grid in a single layer with space between each piece. This will allow the smoke to circulate around all pieces evenly.

8. Place dome lid on smoker and water-smoke. Refer to cooking chart for cooking times. Do not remove dome lid more than is absolutely necessary as this will allow heat and moisture to escape and slow the cooking process. The heat indicator in the dome handle will help you monitor the cooking conditions inside the smoker. The food is cooking properly when heat indicator needle is pointing anywhere in the IDEAL range. If the needle drops to

COOL, you may need to add more charcoal to the fire. If the needle reaches HOT, you may need to add more water to the water pan.

9. Clean water pan and cooking grid(s) after each use. Empty water pan and wash it with warm soapy water. Rinse and dry. Use a stiff wire cleaning brush to clean the grid(s). It may be necessary to soak and wash the grid(s) to remove the more stubborn food remains. If so, use a mild soap and hot water solution. Rinse and dry grid(s) well. Do not use a commercial oven cleaner. ALWAYS DUMP ashes after each cookout. Leaving ashes in the fire pan between uses can cause early deterioration of the pan, especially if ashes become wet. Be sure the fire is completely out before emptying the ashes from the pan.

Additional User Instructions: The smoker body may be lifted off the charcoal fire pan to add charcoal or flavoring wood sticks. When the smoker is in use, extreme care should be taken in removing the smoker body from the fire pan to add charcoal or flavoring wood. Be sure to consider the added weight of the food being cooked and the HOT water in the pan before you attempt to lift it. Being careful not to touch hot surfaces, grasp the side handles firmly and avoid tilting the smoker as you lift it. Careless handling, or tilting of the smoker body, could cause HOT water to spill from the pan and scald feet or legs.

Water may be added to the water pan by removing the dome lid and pouring water down through the cooking grid(s) from the top of the smoker. Replace dome lid.

Charcoal: The cooking quality of charcoal briquettes varies. The one you choose may affect the cooking time and temperature. Hardwood charcoal briquettes make the hottest, longest lasting fire. Select a good quality charcoal and use it for consistent cooking performance. Always close the bag tightly on unused charcoal and store it in a dry place. Charcoal that has gotten damp will not burn well. Older charcoal may not burn as well so use soon after opening.

Grilling

The Cook'n Ca'jun water smoker easily converts to a conventional charcoal grill for cooking steaks, hamburgers and hot dogs. To convert into a grill, simply reposition the base pan (with the charcoal fire pan still inside) on top of the support clips at the top of the smoker body and place a cooking grid directly on top of the fire pan. The dome lid should be left on while grilling to obtain faster and better controlled cooking temperatures.

Cooking Chart
CHARCOAL WATER SMOKING

Meat	Quantity	Charcoal (Amount)	Hot Water (Quarts)	Wood Sticks (Qty.)	Cooking Time (Hrs.)	Meat Thermometer Internal Temp. Or Test For Doneness
BEEF (Also Venison) Rump roast	4-5 lbs.	7-8 lbs.	3-4	2-3	3-4	140°F Rare
Pot roast (arm, chuck, blade, top & bottom round	3-4 lbs.	5-7 lbs.	3	2	2½-3½	160°F Medium 170°F Well Done Well Done may
Short ribs	3-4 lbs. 4-6 lbs.	5-7 lbs. 7-8 lbs.	3 4	2 3	1½-2½ 3-4	require longer cooking times
Brisket	3-4 lbs. 5-7 lbs.	7-8 lbs. 8-10 lbs.	4 5-6	2 3	3-4½ hrs. 4-6½	170°F Well Done
PORK Loin roast, bone-in	3-4 lbs. 5-7 lbs.	8 lbs. 15 lbs.	4 6	2 3	3½-4½ 5-7	170°F Well Done
Loin roast, boneless	3-5 lbs.	10 lbs.	4-5	3	3½-5½	
Spareribs	4-6 lbs. 7-10 lbs.	8-10 lbs. 10 lbs.	4 5-6	3 3	2½-3½ 3½-5	Well Done
Country Style back ribs	4-6 lbs.	7-10 lbs.	5	3	4-5	Meat pulls away from bone
Pork chops 1-inch thick	6-10 chops	5-7 lbs.	3-4	3	2-3	
HAMS Fully-cooked	5-7 lbs.	7-8 lbs.	4	3-4	2½-3½	140°F Well Done
Pre-cooked	8-10 lbs.	10 lbs.	5	3	4-6	160-170°F Well Done
Fresh	16-18 lbs.	15 lbs.	6-7	5	6-8	185°F Well Done
POULTRY Chickens (2 whole) (4 whole)	2-3 lbs. ea. 2-3 lbs. ea.	5-7 lbs. 8-10 lbs.	3-4 4	2 3	2½-3½ 3-4	180°F - Leg moves easily in joint
Hen (one)	5 lbs.	7 lbs.	3	2	3-3½	
Turkey	8-10 lbs. 11-13 lbs. 14-16 lbs.	10 lbs. 12 lbs. 15 lbs.	5 6 8	3 3 4	4-6 6-7½ 6-8	185°F Leg moves easily in joint
LEG OF LAMB	5-7 lbs.	8 lbs.	4-5	3	3½-5	140°F Rare 160°F Medium
VEAL RUMP ROAST	3-5 lbs.	5-7 lbs.	4	2	1½-3½	170°F Well Done
FISH & SEAFOOD Whole fish	4-6 lbs.	7 lbs.	4	2-3	2-3	Flesh white,
Fillets	Full grid	5 lbs.	3	1-2	1½-2½	flakes when
Whole salmon	6-7 lbs.	10 lbs.	5-6	3	4-6½	forked
Shrimp, crab legs, lobster, clams	Full grid	5 lbs.	3	1-2	1-2	Shrimp pink Shells open
WILD GAME Cornish hens	4 hens	5-7 lbs.	3	2	2-3	Leg moves
Small game birds (Quail, dove, squab, etc.)	12-16 birds	7-10 lbs.	4	2-3	2-4	easily in joint
Large game birds (Pheasant, duck, goose, etc.)	5-7 lbs.	8-10 lbs.	4-5	2-3	4-5	180°-185°F Well Done

Allow additional cooking time when outside temperature is colder than 60°F and reduce cooking time when above 80°F. Allow additional cooking time for altitudes above 3500 feet.

Using the Electric Cook'n Ca'jun

Always read the owner's manual for complete instructions on assembling and using your water smoker. Before starting, be prepared by carefully reading the recipe or cooking chart to determine advance preparation needed and cooking times required. Electric water smoking and grilling offers that great outdoor taste with the convenience of electricity. For best results follow these step by step instructions.

1. Remove smoker body from base pan and place water soaked flavoring wood sticks on the bar-b-rok near the element. DO NOT PLACE THE WOOD STICKS DIRECTLY ON THE ELEMENT.

2. Place smoker body back on top of the base pan and remove dome lid. Fill water pan with amount of water recommended in recipe or cooking chart. The use of hot tap water will speed the cooking process. It may be necessary to add water to the pan after about four hours of cooking. Do not allow the water to come in contact with the element.

3. Put cooking grid(s) in place. Place food to be cooked on the grid(s). Arrange meat on the grid(s) in a single layer so there is a little space between each piece. This will allow the smoke and heat to circulate around all pieces evenly.

4. Place dome lid on smoker. Do not remove the dome lid more times than is necessary as this will allow heat and moisture to escape and slow down the cooking process.

5. Plug the power-supply cord of the smoker into an electric outlet. Be sure to use only a properly grounded outlet wired for 115 volts with a current rating of 15 amperes or more. Do not operate other appliances or electric devices on the same supply circuit with the smoker. To do so could overload the circuit and blow a fuse or trip a circuit breaker.

   Do not operate the smoker in the rain or on a damp surface.

   Do not use an ordinary household extension cord with this smoker. Use only a heavy duty 14/3 cord not more than 12 feet long. The longer the cord, the less heat the electric element will produce.

6. Allow food to cook. Refer to recipe or cooking chart for approximate cooking times.

7. Clean water pan and grid(s) after each use. Empty water pan and wash it with warm soapy water. Use a stiff wire cleaning brush to clean the grid(s). It may be necessary to soak and wash the grid(s) to remove the more stubborn stains. If so, use a mild soap and hot water solution. Do not use a commercial oven cleaner. Rinse well and dry water pan and grid(s).

NOTE: Lining the water pan with heavy-duty foil before each use will make for easier clean up. Be sure to cover the entire surface inside the water pan with the foil.

Additional User Instructions: Additional flavoring wood sticks and hot water may be added during the cooking process. To add the wood, unplug the smoker and lift the smoker body off the base pan and set it to one side. Place wood sticks on the bar-b-rok and return body to its original position. Be careful to keep smoker balanced in an upright position when lifting and handling to prevent hot liquids from spilling from the water pan. Visually check to be sure the water pan does not slip out of place when moving the smoker body. Be careful not to touch hot surfaces. Use side handles to lift smoker. To add water, unplug smoker and remove dome lid. Pour water from top down through cooking grid(s). Replace the dome lid and plug in smoker. Add hot tap water so as not to delay cooking time.

Grilling

The Cook'n Ca'jun electric water smoker easily converts to an electric grill for cooking steaks, hamburgers and hot dogs. Simply reposition the base pan (with the bar-b-rok pan and heating element still in place) on top of the support clips at the top of the smoker body. Place a cooking grid directly on top of the base pan. Grill with dome lid on. DO NOT USE WATER TO EXTINGUISH FLARE-UPS. Smother them by placing the dome lid back over the grill.

Cooking Chart
ELECTRIC WATER SMOKING

Meat	Quantity	Hot Water (Quarts)	Wood Sticks (Qty.)	Cooking Time (Hrs.)	Meat Thermometer Internal Temperature Or Test For Doneness
BEEF (Also Venison) Rump Roast	4-5 lbs.	3	2-3	2½-3½	140°F Rare
Pot roast (arm, chuck, blade, top & bottom round)	3-4 lbs.	3	2	2-3	160°F Medium 170°F Well Done
Short ribs	3-4 lbs. 4-6 lbs.	3 4	2 3	1½-2½ 2½-3½	Well Done may require longer cooking times
Brisket	3-4 lbs. 5-7 lbs.	4 4*	2 3	3-4 4-6	170°F Well Done
PORK Loin roast, bone in	3-4 lbs. 5-7 lbs.	4 4*	2 3	3-4 4-6	170°F Well Done
Loin roast, boneless	3-5 lbs.	4*	3	3-5	
Spareribs	4-6 lbs. 7-10 lbs.	4 4*	3 3	2½-3½ 3½-5	Well Done Meat pulls away from bone
Country Style back ribs	4-6 lbs.	4	3	3-4	
Pork chops 1-inch thick	6-10 chops	3-4	2-3	2-3	
HAMS Fully-cooked	5-7 lbs.	3-4	3-4	2-3	140°F Well Done
Pre-cooked	8-10 lbs.	4*	3-4	4-6	160°F-170°F Well Done
Fresh	16-18	4*	5	5½-7½	185°F Well Done
POULTRY Chickens (2 whole) (4 whole)	2-3 lbs. ea. 2-3 lbs. ea.	3-4 4	2 3	2-3 2½-3½	180°F - Leg moves easily in joint
Hen (one)	5 lbs.	3-4	2	2½-3	
Turkey	8-10 lbs. 11-13 lbs. 14-16 lbs.	4* 4* 4*	3 3 4	4-6 5-7 6-8	185°F Leg moves easily in joint
LEG OF LAMB	5-7 lbs.	4*	3	3-5	140°F Rare, 160°F Medium
VEAL RUMP ROAST	3-5 lbs.	4	2	1½-3½	170°F Well Done
FISH & SEAFOOD Whole fish	4-6 lbs.	4	2-3	2-3	Flesh white, flakes when forked
Fillets	Full grid	3	1-2	1½-2½	
Whole salmon	6-7 lbs.	4*	3	4-6½	
Shrimp, crab legs, lobster, clams	Full grid	3	1-2	1-2	Shrimp pink Shells open
WILD GAME Cornish hens	4 hens	3	2	2-3	Leg moves easily in joint
Small game birds (Quail, dove, squab, etc.)	12-16 birds	4	2-3	2-4	
Large game birds (Pheasant, duck, goose, etc.)	5-7	4*	2-3	3½-5	180°F - 185°F Well Done

Allow additional cooking time when outside temperature is below 60°F and reduce cooking time when above 80°F. Allow additional cooking time for altitudes above 3500 feet.

*Add hot tap water after 4 hours or as needed.

Using the Gas Cook'n Ca'jun

Always read the owner's manual for complete instructions on assembling and using your water smoker. Before starting, be prepared by carefully reading the recipe or cooking chart to determine advance preparation needed and cooking time required. Gas water smoking offers that great outdoor taste with the convenience of your indoor gas appliance. No fuss, no muss — simply follow the directions, turn the knob, light the burner and in minutes you're ready to cook. For best results follow these instructions:

1. Remove the dome lid and smoker body from the base pan and set them aside. Following the lighting instructions in your owner's manual, light the gas burner.

2. Place flavoring wood sticks in the top of the heat distribution pan directly above the burner flames. (Sticks should be pre-soaked.)

3. Place the smoker body back on top of the base pan. Place the water pan inside the smoker body and fill with the amount of water recommended in the recipe or cooking chart. It may be necessary to add water after about four hours of cooking.

4. Put cooking grid(s) in place. Place food to be cooked on grid(s). Arrange meat on the grid(s) in a single layer so there is a little space between each piece. This will allow the smoke and heat to circulate around all pieces evenly.

5. Place dome lid on smoker. Set heat control knob and allow the food to cook according to the cooking chart. The heat control setting will vary with outdoor temperatures. In mild or warm weather, set the control knob at a setting about mid-way between "HIGH" and "LOW". During cooler weather (50°F and below) it may be necessary to set the control on the "HIGH" setting. A good rule to follow is to set the heat control knob so the temperature inside the smoker is in the "IDEAL" range on the heat indicator. Avoid taking the dome lid off and on while the food is cooking as this will increase the amount of cooking time.

6. Clean grid(s) and water pan after each use. Empty water pan and wash it with warm soapy water. Use a stiff wire cleaning brush to clean the grid(s). It may be necessary to soak and wash the grid(s) to remove the more stubborn stains. If so, use mild soap and hot water. Do not use a commercial oven cleaner. Rinse grid(s) and water pan well and dry.

Additional User Instructions: Additional hot water and flavoring wood sticks may be added during the cooking process. To add the wood, lift the smoker body off the base pan and set it to one side. Place wood sticks on the heat distribution pan and return body. Be careful to keep smoker balanced in an upright position when lifting and handling, to prevent hot liquids from spilling from the water pan. Also be careful not to touch hot surfaces. Use side handles to lift smoker body. To add water, remove dome lid and pour water from top down through cooking grid(s). Add hot tap water so as not to delay cooking. Replace dome lid.

Grilling

Remove smoker body and dome lid. Place one of the cooking grids direclty on top of the heat distribution pan. Following the lighting instructions, light the burner. With the heat control knob turned to the HIGH position, place the dome lid on top of the grill and allow the grill to preheat for approximately 5 minutes before cooking. The heat control knob may be adjusted to any setting between HIGH and LOW to obtain the desired cooking temperature you want. The dome lid should be left on while grilling to obtain faster and better controlled cooking temperatures.

Cooking Chart
GAS WATER SMOKING

Meat	Quantity	Hot Water (Quarts)	Wood Sticks (Qty.)	Cooking Time (Hrs.)	Meat Thermometer Internal Temperature Or Test For Doneness
BEEF (Also Venison) Rump Roast	4-5 lbs.	4	2-3	3½-5	140°F Rare
Pot roast (arm, chuck, blade, top & bottom round)	3-4 lbs.	3	2	2-3	160°F Medium 170°F Well Done
Short ribs	3-4 lbs. 4-6 lbs.	3 4	2 3	1½-2½ 2½-3½	Well Done may require longer cooking times
Brisket	3-4 lbs. 5-7 lbs.	4 4*	2 3	3-4 4½-6½	170°F Well Done
PORK Loin roast, bone in	3-4 lbs. 5-7 lbs.	4 4*	2 3	3-4 4-6	170°F Well Done
Loin roast, boneless	3-5 lbs.	4*	3	3-5	
Spareribs	4-6 lbs. 7-10 lbs.	4 4*	3 3	2½-3½ 3½-5	Well Done Meat pulls away from bone
Country Style back ribs	4-6 lbs.	4	3	3-4	
Pork chops 1-inch thick	6-10 chops	3	2-3	2-3	
HAMS Fully-cooked	5-7 lbs.	4	3-4	2-3	140°F Well Done
Pre-cooked	8-10 lbs.	4*	3-4	4-6	160°F-170°F Well Done
Fresh	16-18	4*	5	5½-7½	185°F Well Done
POULTRY Chickens (2 whole) (4 whole)	2-3 lbs. ea. 2-3 lbs. ea.	3-4 4	2 3	2-3 2½-3½	180°F - Leg moves easily in joint
Hen (one)	5 lbs.	3	2	2½-3	
Turkey	8-10 lbs. 11-13 lbs. 14-16 lbs.	4* 4* 4*	3 3 4	4-6 5-7 6-8	185°F Leg moves easily in joint
LEG OF LAMB	5-7 lbs.	4*	3	3-5	140°F Rare, 160°F Medium
VEAL RUMP ROAST	3-5 lbs.	4	2	1½-3½	170°F Well Done
FISH & SEAFOOD Whole fish	4-6 lbs.	4	2-3	2-3	Flesh white, flakes when forked
Fillets	Full grid	3	1-2	1½-2½	
Whole salmon	6-7 lbs.	4*	3	4-6½	
Shrimp, crab legs, lobster, clams	Full grid	3	1-2	1-2	Shrimp pink Shells open
WILD GAME Cornish hens	4 hens	3	2	2-3	Leg moves easily in joint
Small game birds (Quail, dove, squab, etc.)	12-16 birds	4	2-3	2-4	
Large game birds (Pheasant, duck, goose, etc.)	5-7	4*	2-3	3½-5	180°F - 185°F Well Done

Allow additional cooking time when the outside temperature is colder than 60°F and reduce cooking time when above 80°F. Allow additional cooking time for altitudes above 3500 feet.

* Add hot tap water after about 4 hours or when needed.

Using These Recipes

The following recipes have been developed for and tested on the Cook'n Ca'jun water smokers. For your convenience, these recipes have been written with water smoke cooking instructions for charcoal and electric smokers. These recipes can also be prepared on the gas smoker using the gas cooking chart for cooking times, amount of water and wood sticks.

These recipes were tested during outside temperatures between 55°F and 75°F. Temperatures above and below this range may affect the cooking times as well as the charcoal and water needed. Always consider other weather conditions such as wind and rain, and make allowances for these in determining the cooking times, the amount of charcoal and water to use.

Hot tap water was used for testing all the recipes. This speeds the cooking process somewhat. You should allow more cooking time when starting with cool tap water. Variations in the amount of water used will also affect the cooking times recommended.

Wood sticks used for testing were approximately 3-inches long and 1-inch thick. The sticks were soaked at least one hour before using in the water smoker. We have found that it takes only a small number of wood sticks to produce an ample smoke flavor.

When only one cooking grid was needed, the top level was used. The food was arranged in a single layer with a small amount of space between pieces. Refrain from removing the dome lid more than necessary as this slows the cooking process.

A high grade of hardwood charcoal was used. There are differences in the burning ability of charcoal and this could slow or speed the cooking process. You will find that the charcoal water smoker gets the hottest during the first hour of cooking. The temperature gradually lowers after this. The larger the amount of charcoal, the slower the temperature decreases.

You will find the cooking temperatures of the electric and gas smokers fairly consistent throughout the cooking process. It is not necessary to preheat the electric and gas smokers since they will reach cooking temperatures quickly.

We hope you will enjoy using the recipes in this cookbook but don't hesitate to experiment and develop your own. Here are some cooking tips to keep in mind:

- Meats should be completely thawed before smoking.
- Meats brought to room temperature will require less cooking time.
- When smoking more than one piece of meat, the cooking time is determined by the largest single piece of meat being cooked.
- Adding large amounts of meat will tend to increase cooking time.

- Marinating meats for several hours will break down the cellular structure, thus the cooking time is generally reduced.
- Save time and money by cooking extra food for freezing. Properly wrap for later oven or microwave heating.
- Brush poultry and naturally lean meats with cooking oil, butter or margarine before cooking.
- Wipe the grids with cooking oil to prevent food from sticking.
- Use a meat thermometer to best determine doneness of large pieces of meat. Insert the probe into the largest muscle of the meat making certain it isn't touching fat or bone.
- Save "water pan stock" for making gravies and soups.

Beef

Please your family, special guest, even the gourmet connoisseur with smoked beef specialties. Water-smoke cooking enhances all cuts of beef from brisket to standing rib roast. One of the delights of water-smoking is that cheaper, less tender cuts of beef can be turned into tasty mouth-watering dishes that will surprise even the picky eaters. Sauces and marinades add special flavors and often serve as tenderizers. Savory Arm Roast, Best Bet Rump Roast, Stuffed Round Steak and Smokey Flank Steak are just a few of the recipes you will enjoy.

Standing Rib Roast

Yield: 12 servings

Onion soup mix gives this roast a toasty onion flavor. Try mesquite flavoring wood for a unique different flavor.

1	5- to 6-pound rib roast	1	envelope onion soup mix
¼	cup oil		Pepper
¼	cup red wine		

Bring roast to room temperature. Combine oil, wine and onion soup mix; let stand for 10 minutes. Pour mixture over roast, making certain top has a covering of onion. Place roast on smoker grid and water-smoke. Use a meat thermometer to determine desired doneness.

Charcoal: Use 8-10 pounds charcoal, 4 quarts hot water, 3 mesquite wood chunks and smoke 4 — 5 hours.

Electric: Use 4 quarts hot water, 3 mesquite wood chunks and smoke 3½ — 4½ hours.

Note: For well done, cooking time may be longer. Add hot water to water pan as needed.

Simple Seasoned Roast

For a delicious easy meal simply use a favorite seasoning on a large beef roast such as rump, sirloin tip, rib roast or large chuck.

Seasonings for beef roast

Seasoned salt	Celery salt and onion salt
Garlic salt or powder	Cajun Barbecue Salt (see note below)
Lemon pepper	Paprika, salt and pepper

Sprinkle roast liberally with any of the above and place on smoker grid. See Cooking Chart for time, water, wood sticks and charcoal. For best results use a meat thermometer.

Note: Recipe in Sauces section.

Standing Rib Roast

Super Roast

Yield: 8 - 10 servings

In this recipe wine and other ingredients are added to the water in the water pan. The flavors will be transmitted to the meat by the steam from the water pan. Try it!!

1 4- to 5-pound boneless beef roast	Seasoned pepper
Oil	2 cups red wine
Garlic salt	2 bay leaves
	1 onion, whole

Wash meat with damp towel and rub with oil. Sprinkle with garlic salt and pepper.

Add bay leaves, onion and wine to hot tap water in the water pan and place pan in smoker. Place roast on smoker grid and insert meat thermometer to best determine desired doneness.

Charcoal: Use 7—8 pounds charcoal, 4 quarts hot water, 2—3 wood sticks and smoke 3—4 hours.
Electric: Use 4 quarts hot water, 2—3 wood sticks and smoke 2½—3½ hours.

Beef Roast Hosun

Yield: 6 - 8 servings

Plan an Oriental menu to go with this roast. Save the marinade to serve with meat as a sauce.

1 3- to 4-pound English cut roast or sirloin tip	1 medium onion, grated
⅓ cup soy sauce	1 clove garlic, minced
¼ cup sherry	2 tablespoons brown sugar
¼ cup pineapple juice	½ teaspoon ginger

Place roast in a plastic bag or in a deep bowl. Combine remaining ingredients and pour over roast. Close bag and turn to coat roast thoroughly with marinade. Refrigerate for several hours or overnight, turning roast occasionally. Place roast fat side up on smoker grid and water-smoke.

Charcoal: Use 5—7 pounds charcoal, 3 quarts hot water, 2 wood sticks and smoke 2½—3½ hours.
Electric: Use 3 quarts hot water, 2 wood sticks and smoke 2—3 hours.

Tipsy Roast

Yield: 8 - 10 servings

Use this marinade on a rolled roast or rump roast bone-in or boneless. Don't forget to use a meat thermometer for desired doneness.

1 4- to 5-pound rump or rolled roast	¼ cup vegetable oil
1 cup red wine	1 tablespoon instant minced onion
¼ cup Pickapeppa sauce, or any steak sauce	1 teaspoon sweet basil leaves
	Garlic salt

Place meat in a plastic or glass dish. Combine wine, Pickapeppa sauce, oil, onion, and basil leaves. Pour mixture over meat and marinate 6 - 8 hours or overnight. Remove meat from marinade and sprinkle with garlic salt. Place roast on smoker grid, insert meat thermometer and water-smoke.

Charcoal: Use 7 — 8 pounds charcoal, 4 quarts hot water, 3 wood sticks and smoke 3 — 4 hours.
Electric: Use 4 quarts hot water, 3 wood sticks and smoke 2½ — 3½ hours.

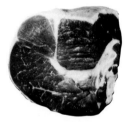

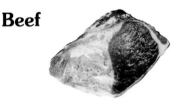

Beef

Beef Bottom Round Roast

Beef Rump Roast

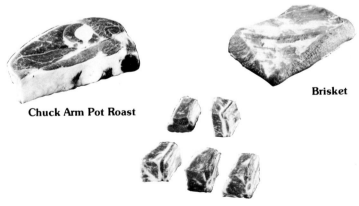

Chuck Arm Pot Roast

Brisket

Short Ribs

Savory Arm Roast

Yield: 6 - 8 servings

Although these roasts do not cook to fork-tenderness on the smoker, they will be more tender if marinated. This tart marinade will tenderize and add a spark of flavor.

1	3- to 4-pound arm or chuck roast	½	teaspoon sweet basil leaves
1	cup Italian salad dressing	½	teaspoon thyme leaves
1	cup beer	½	teaspoon salt
2	bay leaves	½	teaspoon pepper
¾	teaspoon dry mustard		

Combine all ingredients except meat and mix well. Pour mixture over meat. Refrigerate overnight. Remove roast from marinade. Save marinade for later use. Place roast on smoker grid and smoke. Brush with marinade before serving.

Charcoal: Use 5 — 7 pounds charcoal, 3 quarts hot water, 2 wood sticks and smoke 2½ — 3½ hours.
Electric: Use 3 quarts hot water, 2 wood sticks and smoke 2 — 3 hours.

Pranzo di Manzo

Yield: 6 - 8 servings

Fancy name meaning "dinner of beef". Another delightful recipe using your choice of pot roast cuts; chuck, arm, blade or bottom round roast.

1	3- to 4-pound pot roast	2	tablespoons vegetable oil
½	teaspoon salt	2	cups commercial spaghetti sauce
½	teaspoon pepper		

Season meat with salt and pepper. Marinate roast in oil and spaghetti sauce overnight. Remove roast from sauce and place on smoker grid to smoke. Serve sliced with extra sauce.

Charcoal: Use 5 — 7 pounds charcoal, 3 quarts hot water, 2 wood sticks and smoke 2½ — 3½ hours.
Electric: Use 3 quarts hot water, 2 wood sticks and smoke 2 — 3 hours.

Smoked Carne Asada

Yield: 6 - 8 servings

A favorite Mexican dish with a touch of smoke flavor. Use hot peppers in place of bell peppers for an extra spicy flavor.

1 3- to 4-pound pot roast (chuck, arm, or 2-inch thick round steak)	1 large bell pepper, cut in strips
½ cup red wine	1 medium onion, sliced
½ cup beef broth	1 clove garlic, minced
1 can (4 ounces) taco sauce	Dash pepper
2 fresh tomatoes, sliced or 1 cup canned tomatoes, sliced	

Pierce meat in several places with a fork. Combine remainder of ingredients and pour over meat. Marinate meat in sauce for several hours or overnight. Remove meat from sauce and place on smoker grid. Spoon sauce on top of meat omitting vegetables. Add remainder of sauce and vegetables the last 30 minutes of cooking or heat sauce and serve on meat.

Charcoal: Use 5 — 7 pounds charcoal, 3 quarts hot water, 2 wood sticks and smoke 2½ — 3½ hours.
Electric: Use 3 quarts hot water, 2 wood sticks and smoke 2 — 3 hours.

Herbed Roast

Yield: 6 - 8 servings

Tomato juice and herbs give this roast a distinct robust flavor. Other pot roast cuts such as blade or arm roast could be used.

1	3- to 4-pound shoulder chuck or 1 eye of round roast	1	teaspoon pepper
		1	teaspoon rosemary
		1	teaspoon celery seeds
1	tablespoon meat tenderizer	⅛	teaspoon sage
1	cup tomato juice	⅛	teaspoon of thyme
¾	cup vegetable oil	2	onions, sliced
1¾	cup water	2	tablespoons melted margarine or butter
¼	cup lemon juice		
1½	teaspoons salt	2	slices bacon

Pierce surface of meat in several places and sprinkle with meat tenderizer. Mix remaining ingredients except bacon and pour over meat. Let meat stand in marinade 8 - 12 hours in refrigerator. Remove meat from marinade (save) and place on smoker grid. Top meat with bacon slices and baste with marinade. Baste again with marinade after water-smoking.

Charcoal: Use 5 — 7 pounds charcoal, 3 quarts hot water, 2 wood sticks and smoke 2½ — 3½ hours.
Electric: Use 3 quarts hot water, 2 wood sticks and smoke 2 — 3 hours.

Best Bet Rump Roast

Yield: 8 - 10 servings

A marinade will add more flavor if the meat is pierced in several places. You can bet everyone will like this one. Adding cola to the water pan produces extra flavor.

1	4- to 5-pound rump roast or bottom round		Coarse, ground black pepper
	Meat tenderizer	2	bay leaves
1	cup cola	1	tablespoon cloves, whole
1	Envelope dry onion soup mix	1	quart cola

Use a damp towel to wash meat. Pierce meat with a fork in several places and sprinkle with meat tenderizer. Mix together cola and onion soup mix, then pour over roast. Marinate 6 - 8 hours or overnight. Remove roast from marinade and sprinkle with pepper.

Pour remaining marinade into water pan and add bay leaves, cloves and cola. Place roast on smoker grid and water-smoke. For determining desired doneness use a meat thermometer.

Charcoal: Use 7 — 8 pounds charcoal, 2 quarts hot water (see note below), 3 wood sticks and smoke 3 — 4 hours.

Electric: Use 2 quarts hot water (see note below), 3 wood sticks and smoke 2½ — 3½ hours.

Note: Add water in addition to cola and marinade making 3 quarts liquid in water pan.

Stuffed Round Steak

Yield: 6 - 8 servings

This stuffed and rolled steak has a seasoned bread stuffing and is very pretty when sliced. Stuffed round steak has to be tied with string so it will hold together while cooking. Serve with a mushroom gravy.

2 2-pound round steaks	1 cup bread crumbs
Meat tenderizer	⅔ cup fresh parmesan
2 cups fresh mushrooms,	cheese, grated
sliced	¼ cup pimento stuffed
1 small clove garlic, minced	Spanish olives, sliced
¾ cup chopped green onion	½ teaspoon paprika
2 tablespoons vermouth or	¼ teaspoon oregano leaves
sherry	⅛ teaspoon sage
1 teaspoon lemon juice	Salt
2 tablespoons vegetable oil	Pepper
or bacon drippings	Oil
3 tablespoons butter or	String
margarine	

Sprinkle steak with meat tenderizer then pound meat to tenderize. Sauté mushrooms, onions and garlic in butter and oil. Stir in lemon juice and vermouth and cook until soft. Combine remainder of ingredients, except oil, for stuffing. Prepare steaks by overlapping about ¼ to ½ of the steaks. Place stuffing in center (overlapped area) and starting with short side wrap one side around stuffing and bring other side over first. Secure by tieing string around roll in several places so it will tightly hold stuffing. Brush roll with oil and place on smoker grid. Serve with mushroom sauce, canned or homemade.

Charcoal: Use 5 — 7 pounds charcoal, 3 quarts hot water, 2 wood sticks and smoke 2½ hours.

Electric: Use 2½ quarts hot water, 2 wood sticks and smoke 2 hours.

Smoked Meat Loaf

Yield: 6 individual loaves

Making these into individual loaves increases smoke penetration. This is great when smoked and later warmed in a microwave.

1	pound ground pork and 2 pounds ground beef or 1 pound ground beef, 1 pound ground pork, and 1 pound ground veal (total: 3 pounds meat)	2	eggs, beaten
		¾	cup chopped onion
		1	teaspoon beef bouillon
		¼	cup chopped parsley
1	slice white bread, crust removed	½	cup finely chopped celery
		¼	teaspoon poultry seasoning
		¼	teaspoon garlic powder
¼	cup milk	½	teaspoon salt

Tear or crumble the bread and add to the milk. Combine the remaining ingredients, then add the milk mixture and mix well. Shape into 6 loaves. Put loaves on aluminum trays or pieces of foil and place on smoker grid to water-smoke.

Charcoal: Use 5 pounds charcoal, 3 quarts hot water, 2 wood sticks and smoke 1½ – 2 hours.
Electric: Use 2 quarts hot water, 2 wood sticks and smoke 1½ – 2 hours.

Au Gourmet Meat Loaf

Yield: 6 - 8 servings

Au Gourmet Meat Loaf looks like tenderloin but it's really ground beef, bacon wrapped and studded with frankfurters.

1½	pounds ground chuck	1	teaspoon salt
1	medium onion, minced	½	teaspoon pepper
¼	cup finely chopped green pepper	2	tablespoons Worcestershire sauce
½	cup bread crumbs	3	frankfurters
1	egg, beaten	5-6	bacon slices

Combine and mix well all ingredients except frankfurters and bacon slices. On wax paper spread mixture into rectangle approximately 12-inches wide by 10-inches long. Cut each frank in half lengthwise; place each frank half parallel, about 1-inch apart, down length of meat. With aid of wax paper, roll up tightly from short side, jelly roll fashion. Lay 2 bacon slices on top of roll lengthwise; wrap remainder of slices around roll securing ends with toothpicks. Place on smoker grid and water-smoke.

Charcoal: Use 5 pounds charcoal, 3 quarts hot water, 1 – 2 wood sticks and smoke 1 – 1½ hours.
Electric: Use 2 quarts hot water, 1 – 2 wood sticks and smoke 1 – 1½ hours.

Au Gourmet Meat Loaf, Sunshine Bread

Backyard Meat Loaf

Yield: 6 servings

Try smoked meat loaf! This recipe has a super tangy sauce. The loaf will hold its shape better if placed on a small piece of foil.

1½	pounds ground chuck	½	teaspoon pepper
⅓	cup chili sauce or catsup	1	can (8 ounces) tomato sauce
½	cup bread crumbs		
1	egg, beaten	2	tablespoons brown sugar
¼	cup finely chopped green pepper	1	tablespoon prepared mustard
1	tablespoon instant minced onion	1	tablespoon Worcestershire sauce
1	teaspoon salt	2	tablespoons vinegar

Combine ground meat, chili sauce, crumbs, egg, green pepper, onion, salt and pepper. Mix well, form into loaf and place in a shallow pan (8 inch square foil pan). Blend remaining ingredients and pour over loaf. Place uncovered pan on smoker grid and water-smoke.

Charcoal: Use 5 pounds charcoal, 3 quarts hot water, 1 – 2 wood sticks and smoke 1½ – 2 hours.
Electric: Use 2 quarts hot water, 1 – 2 wood sticks and smoke 1½ – 2 hours.

Barbecued Short Ribs

Yield: 4 servings

A simple recipe using commercial barbecue sauce with added flavors. The sauce could be used on bone-in short ribs; just increase cooking time.

3-4	pounds short ribs, boneless or thin sliced	⅓	cup seafood cocktail sauce
1½	cups barbecue sauce	3	tablespoons wine vinegar

Place ribs in a baking dish, bowl or heavy duty plastic bag. Combine other ingredients and pour over ribs. Toss ribs so all are evenly coated. Refrigerate for at least 8 hours or overnight. Remove ribs from sauce and place on smoker grid. Baste with sauce before cooking and once during cooking.

Charcoal: Use 5 – 7 pounds charcoal, 3 quarts hot water, 2 wood sticks and smoke 1½ – 2½ hours.
Electric: Use 2½ quarts hot water, 2 wood sticks and smoke 1½ – 2½ hours.

Herbed Beef Short Ribs

Yield: 6 servings

Serve these herbed beef ribs with gravy made from the delicious drippings in the water pan.

4 to 5	pounds beef short ribs, about 2½-inches thick	2	tablespoons prepared mustard
¼	cup vegetable oil	1	teaspoon garlic powder
⅓	cup red dry wine	1	teaspoon dried dill
⅓	cup vinegar	5-6	drops Tabasco sauce
1	tablespoon Worcestershire sauce		

Put the ribs in a baking dish, bowl or heavy-duty plastic bag. Combine all remaining ingredients and blend well. Pour marinade over ribs. Turn the ribs to coat them completely with the marinade. Cover or seal bag and refrigerate several hours, preferably overnight, turning occasionally. Remove meat from marinade and place on smoker grid to water-smoke.

Charcoal: Use 7 pounds charcoal, 3 quarts hot water, 2 wood sticks and smoke 2½ – 3½ hours.
Electric: Use 3 quarts hot water, 2 wood sticks and smoke 2 – 3 hours.

Smoky Flank Steak

Yield: 4 - 6 servings

Flank steak marinated in a pungent sauce and then smoke-cooked makes a mouth-watering main dish. For tenderness slice on the diagonal and across the grain.

1	1½- to 2-pound flank steak	2	green onions, finely chopped
¾	cup vegetable oil		
3	tablespoons honey	½	teaspoon garlic powder
2	tablespoons vinegar	½	teaspoon ground ginger

Combine all ingredients except steak. Let set for about 1 hour. Pour mixture over steak and marinate overnight. Place steak directly on smoker grid and baste with marinade before and after cooking.

Charcoal: Use 5 pounds charcoal, 3 quarts hot water, 2 wood sticks and smoke 1 – 2 hours.
Electric: Use 2 quarts hot water, 2 wood sticks and smoke 1 – 1½ hours.
Reduce cooking time 30 minutes for rare.

Teriyaki Flank Steak

Yield: 4 servings

Surprisingly, this marinade will tenderize the steak and adds a fantastic flavor. A good marinade to use on brisket also.

1	1½-pound flank steak	⅛	cup Pickapeppa (optional)
¼	cup teriyaki sauce	3	tablespoons red wine,
¼	cup vegetable oil		or red wine vinegar
¼	cup water	2	tablespoons brown sugar
⅛	cup soy sauce	1	clove garlic, minced

Pierce steak on both sides with fork. Combine remaining ingredients and pour over steak. Cover and marinate overnight, turning occasionally. Remove steak from marinade and place on smoker grid.

Charcoal: Use 5 pounds charcoal, 3 quarts hot water, 2 wood sticks and smoke 1 hour.
Electric: Use 2 quarts hot water, 2 wood sticks and smoke 1 hour.

Smoked Calf Liver

Yield: 4 - 6 servings

Liver and onions smoked are really special. Bacon on top keeps the liver from cooking dry.

	1-2 pounds calf liver	1	large onion, sliced
	Worcestershire sauce	½	cup canned, sliced
	Hickory salt		mushrooms
3	tablespoons bacon		Bacon
	drippings		

Coat liver with Worcestershire sauce, sprinkle with hickory salt and refrigerate until onion mixture is ready. Sauté onion in oil until soft, then add mushrooms. Cool onion mixture. Place one slice of the liver on a double thickness of heavy-duty foil, greased. Spread onion mixture over liver, then place another slice of liver on top of onions. Lay uncooked bacon slices on top of liver. Place liver on smoker grid and smoke.

Charcoal: Use 5 pounds charcoal, 3 quarts hot water, 2 wood sticks and smoke 1 — 2 hours.
Electric: Use 3 quarts hot water, 2 wood sticks and smoke 1 — 2 hours.

Marinated Brisket

Yield: 6 - 8 servings

A simple marinade for a small brisket. Be sure to cut thin slices, at a slant, across the grain of the meat.

1 3- to 4-pound brisket (see note below) Meat tenderizer	2 cups Italian salad dressing 1 teaspoon chili powder

Sprinkle meat thoroughly with meat tenderizer and let set 5 - 10 minutes. Combine Italian dressing and chili powder for marinade. Pour over brisket and marinate overnight. Remove brisket from marinade and water-smoke.

Charcoal: Use 7— 8 pounds charcoal, 4 quarts hot water, 2 wood sticks and smoke 3— 4½ hours.
Electric: Use 4 quarts hot water, 2 wood sticks and smoke 3— 4 hours.
Note: For a 5— pound brisket use 8— 10 pounds charcoal and increase smoking time (charcoal and electric) 1 to 1½ hours.

The most popular meat is beef. Even less expensive beef cuts can be successfully smoked. Rump, chuck, blade, round, sirloin tip and brisket are equally succulent. Select the best possible grade of meat, only USDA prime and choice grades are recommended. Prime and choice beef are of top quality with bright red meat and firm white fat. As the grade gets lower, the red of the meat deepens and the fat takes on a yellowish cast.

Pan Cooked Brisket

Yield: 6 servings

This brisket is smoked in a foil roasting pan and topped with a thick sauce. Try this recipe for a more tender brisket.

1 2½- to 3½-pound brisket, trimmed 1 jar (12 ounces) chili sauce	1 envelope dry onion soup mix ½ cup water

Combine chili sauce, onion soup mix, ½ cup water and mix well. Place meat in a foil roaster pan no larger than 11⅝ × 9¼ × 2⅜ inches. Pour ½ cup water in roaster pan. Spread sauce over meat and place roaster pan with brisket on smoker grid.

Charcoal: Use 7— 8 pounds charcoal, 4 quarts hot water, 3 wood sticks and smoke 3½ — 4½ hours.
Electric: Use 4 quarts hot water, 3 wood sticks and smoke 3— 4 hours.

Smoked Corned Beef

Yield: 6 - 8 servings

This makes especially good sandwiches, hot or cold.

1	2½- to 3½-pound corned beef brisket	1	large bay leaf, broken into pieces
¼	cup water	½	teaspoon peppercorns
1	clove garlic, chopped		

Tear off an 18-inch piece of heavy-duty foil. Fold up edges slightly, making a drip pan, or use a foil pan. Remove corned beef brisket from its wrapping. Rinse thoroughly and place the brisket in center of foil. Combine water and seasonings and pour over brisket. Place the brisket in the foil pan on the smoker grid and water-smoke.

Charcoal: Use 7−8 pounds charcoal, 4 quarts hot water, 2−3 wood sticks and smoke 3½−4½ hours.
Electric: Use 4 quarts hot water, 2−3 wood sticks and smoke 3−4 hours.

Italian Stuffed Peppers

Yield: 4 - 5 servings

Everyone likes stuffed peppers so try this one on your family.

4-5	large green peppers	½	can (8 ounce) tomato sauce
1	pound ground chuck	½	cup finely chopped onion
¾	cup bread crumbs		
½	cup grated Romano cheese	½	teaspoon garlic salt
1	egg, beaten	½	teaspoon chopped parsley

Wash peppers well and cut a slice from stem end, remove seeds and membrane. Combine remaining ingredients and stuff peppers with meat mixture. Place peppers in a baking pan, foil pan or double thickness of heavy-duty foil. Top peppers with remaining tomato sauce and place on smoker grid to water-smoke.

Charcoal: Use 5 pounds charcoal, 3 quarts hot water, 1 wood stick and smoke 1½−2 hours.
Electric: Use 2 quarts hot water, 1 wood stick and smoke 1½−2 hours.

Pork

The "little pig who goes to market" saw America first some 400 years ago with the Spanish explorer, DeSoto. The "little pig" is at its best when smoked and with a water smoker you can create such succulent delights as Italian Stuffed Pork Roast, Deviled Pork Chops, Smoked Tenderloin, Smoked Fresh Ham, Plum Good Ribs and Teutonic Pork Shoulder Roast. Pork requires longer cooking times and it would be a good idea to use a meat thermometer when smoking large cuts. Ham is a prime favorite and is available in a variety of types — fully-cooked, cook-before-eating, canned and fresh. These ham types require different cooking times so know your ham.

Southern Spareribs

Yield: 4 - 6 servings

Pork at its best! For this one you will need to use both grids. Ribs on the top grid will cook faster.

4-6	pounds pork spareribs	3	tablespoons soy sauce
1	cup catsup	1	teaspoon salt
½	cup brown sugar	1	cup Dr. Pepper
¼	cup honey		

Pierce meaty parts of ribs with a fork. Mix well all ingredients except ribs. Soak ribs in marinade 5-7 hours or overnight. Remove from marinade and place on smoker grid or in a rib rack on the grid.

Charcoal: Use 8 pounds charcoal, 4 quarts hot water, 3 wood sticks and smoke 2½ — 3½ hours.
Electric: Use 3 — 4 quarts hot water, 3 wood sticks and smoke 2½ — 3½ hours.

Special Smoked Ribs

Yield: 4 - 6 servings

With the use of a rib rack you can smoke a larger quantity of ribs. Ribs on the top grid will probably cook faster.

4-6	pounds pork spareribs	2	tablespoons chili powder
2	cans (8 ounces) tomato sauce	2	teaspoons paprika
½	cup vinegar	2	teaspoons salt
½	cup brown sugar	1	tablespoons celery seed
2	tablespoons Worcestershire sauce		

Cut ribs in 5-6 rib sections and set aside. Combine remaining ingredients in a saucepan and heat until sugar melts and mixture is well blended. Pour mixture over ribs and marinate 5-7 hours. Remove ribs from mixture and place on smoker grid or in a rib rack on the grid. Brush with mixture once again before smoking.

Charcoal: Use 7 — 8 pounds charcoal, 4 quarts hot water, 3 wood sticks and smoke 2½ — 3½ hours.
Electric: Use 3 — 4 quarts hot water, 3 wood sticks and smoke 2½ — 3½ hours.

**Southern Spareribs, Smoked Sausage
and Maple Glazed Ham decorated**

Orange Flavored Spareribs

Yield: 6 - 8 servings

A hint of orange gives these ribs a citrus tangy flavor.

6-7	pounds pork spareribs	½	cup brown sugar
2	cups barbecue sauce	1	tablespoon grated
1	cup ginger ale or beer		orange peel
½	cup fresh orange juice	½	teaspoon garlic powder
¼	cup lemon juice	1	tablespoon instant
¼	cup teriyaki sauce		minced onion

Cut ribs in 5 — 6 rib sections. Combine all ingredients and pour over ribs. Let ribs soak in sauce overnight. Remove ribs from sauce and place on smoker grids. Remember, ribs on top rack will probably cook faster and brown more. Place ribs on smoker grid or in a rib rack on the grid and water-smoke.

Charcoal: Use 7 — 8 pounds charcoal, 4 quarts hot water, 3 wood sticks and smoke 3 — 4 hours.
Electric: Use 3 — 4 quarts hot water, 3 wood sticks and smoke 3 — 4 hours.

Bavarian Ribs and Kraut

Yield: 6 - 8 servings

Meat and vegetables are all cooked on the smoker in this recipe.

6-7	pounds spareribs	1	tablespoon caraway seed
2	1-pound cans sauerkraut	8	or more small, whole
½	cup chopped onion		new potatoes
1	cup white wine	1	quart hot water
2	tablespoons brown sugar		

Remove the ribs from the refrigerator an hour or so before smoking so they will be at room temperature. Place ribs on the smoker grid or in a rib rack on the grid and water-smoke.

Meanwhile, combine the sauerkraut, onion and all the remaining ingredients and place in an oven-proof casserole dish or foil pan. After about 2 hours place the sauerkraut mixture and potatoes, uncovered, on lower grid. Add more hot water to the water pan if needed. Smoke cook an additional 1½-2 hours. Check casserole dish after 1 hour, adding more water if necessary.

Charcoal: Use 8 — 10 pounds charcoal, 4 quarts hot water, 2 wood sticks and smoke 3½ — 4½ hours.
Electric: Use 3 — 4 quarts hot water, 2 wood sticks and smoke 3½ — 4½ hours.

Lemon-Dill Back Ribs

Yield: 6 servings

Back ribs, often called country style ribs, are very meaty and perfect for water-smoking.

4 pounds back ribs (country style)	½ teaspoon dried dillweed or caraway seed
3 lemons	¼ teaspoon basil
Lemon peel, grated	2 drops red pepper sauce
1 teaspoon sugar	
1 teaspoon oil	
¼ teaspoon salt	

Arrange the ribs in a baking dish or in a heavy-duty plastic bag. Grate the peel from 1 of the lemons and reserve. Juice all 3 lemons. Combine grated lemon peel, juice and all the remaining ingredients in a small bowl and pour over the ribs. Cover with plastic wrap or close the bag securely and marinate for about 1 hour at room temperature. Place ribs on smoker grid and place in smoker. Pour the marinade over the ribs and let drip into the water pan.

Charcoal: Use 7 — 8 pounds charcoal, 4 quarts hot water, 2 — 3 wood sticks and smoke 3½ — 4 hours.
Electric: Use 3 — 4 quarts hot water, 2 — 3 wood sticks and smoke 2½ — 3 hours.

Plum Good Ribs

Yield: 4 servings

A lot of plum jam and a little whiskey produces a very good flavor for country ribs.

3-4 pounds country style back ribs	1 tablespoon lemon juice
¾ cup plum jam	1 tablespoon grated onion
¾ cup barbecue sauce	¼ teaspoon grated fresh ginger
¼ cup whiskey	

Pierce meaty portion of ribs with a fork. Mix other ingredients in a saucepan and heat until jam is melted. Pour mixture over ribs and marinate overnight. Remove ribs and place on smoker grid. Heat remaining sauce and serve hot with ribs.

Charcoal: Use 7 — 8 pounds charcoal, 4 quarts hot water, 2 wood sticks and smoke 3 — 4 hours.
Electric: Use 3 — 4 quarts hot water, 2 wood sticks and smoke 2 — 3 hours.

Chinese Country Ribs

Yield: 4 - 6 servings

Country style ribs, called back ribs, or backbone in some regions. These ribs are meaty and you will need half as many as spareribs.

3-4	pounds country-style back ribs	3	tablespoons sherry
½	cup orange marmalade	1	clove garlic, minced
¼	cup soy sauce	2	teaspoons Hoisin sauce
¼	cup catsup	¼	teaspoon finely grated, fresh ginger
3	tablespoons chili sauce	1	tablespoon cornstarch

Ribs will retain more flavor from sauce if soaked in sauce overnight. Combine all ingredients in a saucepan and heat slowly until well blended and thickened. Cool sauce and pour over ribs. When ready to smoke place ribs on smoker grid and brush with sauce. Brush again before serving.

Charcoal: Use 7 – 8 pounds charcoal, 4 quarts hot water, 2 wood sticks and smoke 3 – 4 hours.
Electric: Use 3 – 4 quarts hot water, 2 wood sticks and smoke 2 – 3 hours.

Snappy Butterfly Pork Chops

Yield: 4 - 6 servings

English mustard gives these chops a real tart and snappy flavor. Soak the chops in the sauce to enhance the flavor.

4-6	¾- to 1-inch thick pork chops, butterfly cut	⅓	cup orange juice
	English mustard	¼	cup catsup
⅔	cup honey	1	small clove garlic, minced

Spread both sides of pork chops with English mustard. Combine remainder of ingredients and mix well. Place chops in sauce and soak 4-6 hours turning occasionally. Remove chops from sauce and place on smoker grid. Pour sauce over chops and smoke.

Charcoal: Use 5 pounds charcoal, 3 quarts hot water, 2 wood sticks and smoke 2 – 2½ hours.
Electric: Use 3 quarts hot water, 2 wood sticks and smoke 1½ – 2 hours.

Deviled Pork Chops

Yield: 6 servings

Save some of this sauce to heat and serve with chops. Smoke these chops with other meats to save time and energy.

6	1-inch thick pork chops	4	tablespoons prepared mustard
½	cup chili sauce	1	teaspoon salt
½	cup catsup	½	teaspoon oregano leaves
2	tablespoons Worcestershire sauce	⅛	teaspoon cayenne pepper

Set pork chops aside and combine other ingredients. Spread sauce on both sides of chops and let set in sauce at least 1 hour. Place chops on smoker grid and spread tops with sauce. Heat any remaining sauce and serve with chops. Prepare smoker and water-smoke.

Charcoal: Use 5 pounds charcoal, 3 quarts hot water, 2 wood sticks and smoke 2 – 2½ hours.
Electric: Use 3 quarts hot water, 2 wood sticks and smoke 1½ – 2 hours.

Sausage Stuffed Pork Chops

Yield: 6 servings

These thick meaty pork chops are stuffed with spicy sausage and rice. Plan one chop per person.

6	1½-inch thick pork chops, with pocket	½	cup chopped green onion
	Salt and pepper	½	cup canned sliced mushrooms
1	cup white rice, cooked	¼	teaspoon ground sage
1	pound pork sausage	1	teaspoon dry mustard

Season pork chops with salt and pepper. Cook sausage in a skillet until brown, then add onions and mushrooms and cook until soft. Stir in remaining ingredients and mix thoroughly. Fill each chop with stuffing and place on smoker grid. Prepare smoker and water smoke chops.

Charcoal: Use 5 pounds charcoal, 3 quarts hot water, 2 wood sticks and smoke 2 – 2½ hours.
Electric: Use 3 quarts hot water, 2 wood sticks and smoke 1½ – 2 hours.

Fruity Stuffed Pork Chops

Yield: 3 servings

These apple flavored and apple stuffed chops will please all hearty appetites.

3 ¾-inch pork chops, with pocket	½ cup chopped apple
1 cup apple juice	¼ cup white raisins
4 slices bread, crumbled	⅛ teaspoon pepper
1 tablespoon chopped onion	⅛ teaspoon sage
	1 egg, beaten

Marinate the pork chops in the apple juice for a half hour. Mix the remaining ingredients and stuff into the pocket of pork chops. Place pork chops on smoker grid and smoke.

Charcoal: Use 5 pounds charcoal, 3 quarts hot water, 1 wood stick and smoke 2 – 2½ hours.
Electric: Use 3 quarts hot water, 1 wood stick and smoke 1½ – 2 hours.

Mince Pork Chops

Yield: 6 servings

If you like mincemeat you will love these stuffed pork chops.

6 1½-inch pork chops, with pocket	½ cup orange juice
1 package (9 ounces) mincemeat	1 tablespoon sherry
	1 tablespoon honey
	1 teaspoon ground ginger

Place mincemeat in a saucepan and stir in orange juice. Heat and stir until well blended. Turn off heat and add remaining ingredients, mixing well. Stuff each chop with mincemeat mixture and place on smoker grid. Prepare smoker and water-smoke.

Charcoal: Use 5 pounds charcoal, 3 quarts hot water, 2 wood sticks and smoke 2 – 2½ hours.
Electric: Use 3 quarts hot water, 2 wood sticks and smoke 1½ – 2 hours.

For stuffed chops, have the butcher cut the chops thick. To make a pocket, slice the lean part of the meat in half, cutting to the bone. Fill the chops with stuffing; tie chops to hold in stuffing.

So-Simple Stuffed Pork Chops

Yield: 4 - 6 servings

Sliced onions really flavor these chops and the preparation is so simple.

4-6 1½-inch pork chops, with pocket	1 green pepper, cut in strips
2 onions, sliced ¼-inch thick	1 jar (2 ounces) chopped pimentos
	Barbecue or seasoned salt

Fill each pork chop first with onion slice, green pepper strips and chopped pimentos. Season chops on both sides with barbecue salt and place on smoker grid. Prepare smoker and smoke.

Charcoal: Use 5 pounds charcoal, 3 quarts hot water, 2 wood sticks and smoke 2 — 2½ hours.
Electric: Use 3 quarts hot water, 2 wood sticks and smoke 1½ — 2 hours.

PORK

Pork Shoulder Arm Roast

Pork Loin Roast (Center Cut)

Pork Top Loin Roast (Boneless and Rolled)

Pork Spareribs

Pork Loin Butterfly Chops

Smoked Barbecued Pork Roast

Yield: 7 - 9 servings

Leftovers make fantastic sandwiches. You may wish to smoke more than one roast and freeze for future meals. Definitely use a meat thermometer on all pork roasts to determine doneness.

1 3- to 4-pound boneless rolled pork roast	Barbecue sauce Chopped parsley

Brush the roast generously with barbecue sauce and sprinkle with chopped parsley. Insert meat thermometer and place on smoker grid. Smoke until meat thermometer reaches 170°F.

Charcoal: Use 10 pounds charcoal, 4 — 5 quarts hot water, 3 wood sticks and smoke 3½ — 4½ hours.
Electric: Use 4 quarts hot water, 3 wood sticks and smoke 3 — 4 hours.

Teutonic Pork Shoulder Roast

Yield: 6 servings

For a perfect German touch serve with slices of light and dark rye bread, German cheese slices, crisp cauliflowerettes and buttered asparagus with hot German potato salad.

1 3- to 4-pound pork shoulder roast Salt and pepper 2¼ cups warm beer	1 cup packed brown sugar 1 teaspoon dry mustard ¼ cup bread crumbs

Wash roast, pat dry and season with salt and pepper. Marinate in 2 cups beer for 3 to 4 hours. Combine brown sugar, bread crumbs, dry mustard and remaining ¼ cup beer and stir until well blended. Remove roast from marinade and spread brown sugar mixture over roast pressing mixture into roast. Insert meat thermometer, place roast on smoker grid and water-smoke.

Charcoal: Use 10 pounds charcoal, 4 — 5 quarts hot water, 3 wood sticks and smoke 3½ — 4½ hours or until meat thermometer reaches 170° F.
Electric: Use 4 quarts hot water, 3 wood sticks and smoke 3 — 4 hours or until meat thermometer reaches 170° F.

Luau Pork Roast

Yield: 8 servings

This pork loin roast is served with a snappy horseradish sauce. Decorate the platter with parsley and serve with baked sweet potatoes.

1	5-pound pork loin roast	1	clove garlic, finely chopped
4	jars (4¾ ounces) strained apricot baby food	½	teaspoon seasoned pepper
⅓	cup honey	1	tablespoon grated lemon rind
¼	cup soy sauce	½	teaspoon horseradish
¼	cup lemon juice		Parsley
1	cup lemon-lime soda		
4	green onions, thinly sliced		

Wash and pat meat dry. Combine THREE jars strained apricots, honey, soy sauce, lemon juice, lemon-lime soda, onions, garlic and pepper. Pour over roast and marinate in glass dish overnight. Remove roast from marinade, place on smoker grid, brush with marinade, insert meat thermometer and smoke. While meat is cooking, prepare sauce by combining the other jar of apricots with lemon rind and horseradish. Serve sauce with Luau Pork Roast.

Charcoal: Use 10 pounds charcoal, 5 quarts hot water, 3 wood sticks and smoke 4½ − 5½ hours or until meat thermometer reaches 170° F.

Electric: Use 4 quarts hot water, 3 wood sticks and smoke 4 − 5 hours or until meat thermometer reaches 170° F.

Note: Add hot water to water pan after 4 hours if needed.

Boneless Pork Loin Roast With Honey-Mustard Sauce

Yield: 8 servings

1	4-pound boneless pork loin roast	¼	cup Dijon mustard
¾	cup honey		Salt and pepper

Brush pork roast with honey-mustard mixture. Season with salt and pepper and place on smoker grid. Insert meat thermometer and water-smoke.

Charcoal: Use 10 pounds charcoal, 4 − 5 quarts hot water, 3 wood sticks and smoke 4 − 4½ hours or until thermometer reaches 170° F.

Electric: Use 4 quarts hot water, 3 wood sticks and smoke 3½ − 4 hours or until meat thermometer reaches 170° F.

Bohemian Pork Roast

Yield: 8 servings

This roast is a complete meal, great for the busy person.

1	5-pound pork loin roast, bone in	1	cup dry white wine or apple juice
2	pounds sauerkraut	1	tablespoon caraway seed
2	apples, cored and chopped	½	teaspoon celery salt
5	slices bacon, cut into 1-inch pieces	1	quart hot water (or more)

Insert a meat thermometer into the center of the largest muscle of the roast. Make certain the thermometer doesn't touch the bone. Place the meat in the center of the smoker grid. Cover and water-smoke until meat thermometer reaches 170°F. See cooking instructions below.

In the meantime, combine the sauerkraut, apples, bacon, wine and seasonings; set aside. After about 2½-hours, remove the water pan and add the sauerkraut mixture with 1 quart of hot water. Return the water pan with the sauerkraut mixture to the smoker, replace the meat and continue cooking. Check the sauerkraut after 2 hours to make sure it hasn't dried out. Add more wine or water as needed.

Charcoal: Use 10 pounds charcoal, 5 quarts hot water, 3 wood sticks and smoke 4½ – 5½ hours.
Electric: Use 4 quarts hot water, 3 wood sticks and smoke 4 – 5 hours.

Note: Add hot water to water pan after 4 hours if needed.

Florida Pork

Yield: 6 servings

Florida Pork is a fit name for this roast with its orange-flavored stuffing and glaze. Make certain your butcher gives you a center cut with ribs.

1	8- to 12-chop pork loin, center cut with ribs (6-8 pounds)	1	package (8 ounces) ready-mix bread stuffing
½	cup butter or margarine	½	cup orange juice
¾	cup sliced green onions	½	cup honey
1¼	cups orange juice	2	tablespoons steak sauce

Trim excess fat from roast and make slits between chops, about 2 inches deep. Sauté green onions in butter or margarine in a large saucepan; add water and 1¼ cup orange juice. Bring to a boil and remove saucepan from heat. Stir in stuffing mix until well blended. Pack stuffing into pockets in pork roast. Combine ½ cup orange juice, honey and steak sauce in a small saucepan and heat until bubbly. Brush roast and stuffing with mixture. Brush again during smoking and before serving. Place roast on smoker grid and smoke according to instructions below.

Charcoal: Use 10 pounds charcoal, 5 quarts hot water, 3 wood sticks and smoke 4 — 5 hours or until meat thermometer reaches 170° F.

Electric: Use 4 quarts hot water, 3 wood sticks and smoke 3½ — 4½ hours or until meat thermometer reaches 170° F.

NOTE: Add hot water to water pan after 4 hours if needed.

Pork Loin in Wine

Yield: 6 - 8 servings

The red wine in this recipe adds a unique and divine flavor to the pork loin roast.

1	3- to 4-pound pork loin roast	1	clove garlic, minced
¼	cup chopped parsley	2	cups red wine
¼	cup chopped onion		Salt, pepper, sage, and nutmeg
1	bay leaf		

Place roast in a glass dish or heavy-duty plastic bag. Combine parsley, onion, bay leaf, garlic and red wine; pour over roast. Marinate roast in wine marinade overnight. Remove roast from marinade and pat dry. Sprinkle with salt, pepper, sage and nutmeg. Insert meat thermometer into roast and place roast on smoker grid. Pour remaining marinade in water pan and cook roast to 170°F.

Charcoal: Use 10 pounds charcoal, 4 — 5 quarts hot water, 3 wood sticks and smoke 3½ — 4½ hours or until meat thermometer reaches 170° F.

Electric: Use 4 quarts hot water, 3 wood sticks and smoke 3 — 4 hours or until meat thermometer reaches 170° F.

For best results use a meat thermometer when cooking large cuts of fresh pork. An internal temperature of 170°F is recommended by the National Livestock and Meat Board. Insert the thermometer into the thickest meaty section and make certain the end is not resting in fat or on a bone. Pork offers such a variety and is delicious smoked!

Italian Stuffed Pork Roast

Yield: 8 servings

Stuff a rolled pork loin roast with your favorite Italian sausage and top with spaghetti sauce for a superb treat.

1	3- to 4-pound boneless, rolled pork loin roast	1	pound Italian sausage
	Garlic salt	1	jar (10 ounces) spaghetti sauce

Cut string on rolled roast and spread open. Sprinkle the entire roast with garlic salt. Spread center of each half with spaghetti sauce. Place Italian sausage with or without casing on center of bottom half of roast. Place top half on sausage and bottom half of roast. Retie roast very tight and secure, keeping sausage in the center. Spread outside of roast with spaghetti sauce and place in refrigerator for 1-2 hours. Remove roast from refrigerator and place on smoker grid. Add more sauce on top of roast, insert meat thermometer into meat of roast and water-smoke until thermometer reaches 170°F.

Charcoal: Use 10 pounds charcoal, 4 — 5 quarts hot water and smoke 3½ — 4½ hours.
Electric: Use 4 quarts hot water, 3 wood sticks, and smoke 3 — 4 hours.

Glazed Pork Loin

Yield: 6 servings

Although not as easy to carve as a rolled pork roast, you'll find the bone adds considerable flavor to the meat.

1	3- to 4-pound pork loin roast, bone in	½	cup barbecue sauce
1	cup pineapple preserves	1	teaspoon dry mustard
⅔	cup catsup	¼	teaspoon ground cloves

Trim fat on roast to ¼ inch thick. Combine remaining ingredients in a sauce pan and heat until well blended. Brush or pour glaze over roast saving half of glaze. Brush remainder of glaze on roast during last hour of smoking. For best results use a meat thermometer. Place roast on smoker grid and smoke-cook to 170°F.

Charcoal: Use 10 pounds charcoal, 4 — 5 quarts hot water, 3 wood sticks and smoke 3½ — 4½ hours.
Electric: Use 4 quarts hot water, 3 wood sticks and smoke 3 — 4 hours.

Smoked Pork Tenderloin

Yield: 2 - 4 servings

A lean succulent pork roast. Great for cold sandwiches. Cook two in the same amount of time and freeze one for later.

1	1½- to 2-pound pork tenderloin	1	teaspoon Hoisin sauce
1	cup apricot nectar	1	clove garlic, minced
½	cup apple cider or apricot brandy	1	tablespoon brown sugar
2	tablespoons soy sauce	½	teaspoon allspice
2	teaspoons vinegar	¼	teaspoon ground ginger
		1	tablespoon whole cloves

Pierce meat with a fork in several places. In a saucepan combine remaining ingredients and heat until sugar is dissolved. Cool. Place meat in a marinating dish or heavy-duty plastic bag and add marinade. Refrigerate overnight in marinade. Remove meat from marinade and place on smoker grid. Pour remaining marinade into water pan.

Charcoal: Use 5 pounds charcoal, 3 quarts hot water, 2 wood sticks and smoke 2½ — 3½ hours.

Electric: Use 3 quarts hot water, 2 wood sticks and smoke 2 — 3 hours.

The fat of pork indicates quality and is largely responsible for the desirable flavor of this meat. In high quality pork, the exterior is well-covered with a layer of fairly firm white fat. The color of the meaty part of young pork is grayish pink, turning to a delicate rose color in older animals. The meat is well-marbled with fat and the texture is firm and fine grained.

Types of Ham

Fully-cooked hams can be eaten without cooking or they may be heated and smoked for extra flavor.

Pre-cooked hams or "cook-before-eating" hams are mildly cured and come partially cooked. They must be cooked again before eating, but for a much shorter time than country hams or fresh ham.

Country hams are sold cured in a variety of ways. A well-aged country ham that is cured with a good deal of salt must be soaked for 12-24 hours, then simmered in water before smoking.

Picnic hams are shoulder cuts which come in pre-cooked (cook-before-eating) or fully-cooked forms. Pre-cooked needs to be cooked longer and fully-cooked can be heated or served cold.

Fresh ham is the hind leg of pork that has not been cured and is uncooked.

Maple Glazed Ham

Yield: 10 - 12 servings

Use a fully-cooked whole, shank or butt ham increasing cooking time for larger whole ham. If a country ham is used soak it in water or apple cider (for a sweet flavor) a few hours or overnight to remove some of the salty taste.

1	5- to 7-pound fully-cooked bone-in ham (shank or butt)	½	teaspoon allspice
1½	cups maple syrup	12-16	whole cloves
1	teaspoon ginger		Pineapple slices, canned
¼	teaspoon nutmeg		Marachino cherries

Remove thick skin if a stronge smoke flavor is desired. Trim fat leaving no more than ½ inch thick covering. Score ham. Combine syrup, ginger, nutmeg and allspice. Place ham in a lage dish and baste with syrup mixture. Let the ham stand in syrup for 1 to 2 hours or until it reaches room temperature; baste frequently with syrup. When ready to smoke, remove ham from dish, stud with cloves and place on smoker grid. Baste with syrup at least twice while smoking. Before last hour of smoking decorate with canned pineapple slices and cherries, baste again. If using a meat thermometer, fully cooked ham should reach an internal temperature of from 130°F to 140°F. Make certain the thermometer is not touching the bone.

Charcoal: Use 7 – 8 pounds charcoal, 3 quarts hot water, 3 – 4 wood sticks and smoke 2½ – 3½ hours.
Electric: Use 3 quarts hot water, 3 – 4 wood sticks and smoke 2 – 3 hours.

Smoked Burgundy Ham

Soaking the ham in burgundy, port or red wine will greatly improve the flavor and tenderness of a bone-in ham. The wine removes any trace of salt from the ham and leaves it fork-tender and very sweet.

1 ham, whole, half or picnic (pre-cooked)	Pineapple juice
1 cup brown sugar	1 teaspoon ginger
1½ teaspoons dry mustard	1 teaspoon ground cloves

Score ham, place on smoker grid and smoke according to cooking charts. Mix brown sugar, mustard, ginger and cloves, adding enough pineapple juice to make a rather thick paste. Forty-five minutes before end of cooking time coat ham with brown sugar mixture and continue smoking.

See cooking charts for smoking instructions.

Marinated and Glazed Canned Ham

Yield: 10 servings

Keep a canned ham on hand for unexpected guests. Bubbles in ginger ale give ham a special flavor. Try a marinade of beer, cola or Dr. Pepper.

1 5-pound canned ham	1 tablespoon cider vinegar
1 bottle ginger ale (10 ounces)	2 teaspoons Dijon mustard
½ cup orange marmalade	8-10 whole cloves
2 tablespoons soy sauce	

Place ham in shallow glass dish and pour ginger ale over ham. Cover and place in refrigerator overnight, turning occasionally. Combine other ingredients in a saucepan and heat until well blended. Spread sauce over ham and place on smoker grid to smoke. Heat any extra sauce and serve on smoked ham.

Charcoal: Use 5 pounds charcoal, 3 quarts hot water, 2 — 3 wood sticks and smoke 2½ — 3 hours.
Electric: Use 3 quarts hot water, 2 — 3 wood sticks and smoke 2 — 2½ hours.

Ham With Cinnamon Peach Glaze

Yield: 10 servings

Try this recipe using a canned ham or a thick, center-cut, fully-cooked ham slice. Since you will be using a fully cooked ham you will be enjoying this tasty recipe after a very short cooking time.

1	5-pound canned ham	2	tablespoons brown sugar
1	package (16 ounce) frozen	1	teaspoon lemon juice
	peach slices, thawed	½	teaspoon cinnamon
¼	cup water or rum		

Place ham on smoker grid and smoke according to time recommended below. Spoon glaze over ham during last one-half hour of the cooking time. To prepare glaze, combine all ingredients in a small saucepan and bring to a boil. Reduce heat and simmer 5 minutes to blend flavors. Serve any remaining glaze with ham.

Charcoal: Use 5 pounds charcoal, 3 quarts hot water, 2 — 3 wood sticks and smoke 2½ — 3 hours.
Electric: Use 3 quarts hot water, 2 — 3 wood sticks and smoke 2 — 2½ hours.

Ham Slices With Pie Filling

Yield: 8 servings

A simple to make topping using canned pie filling gives this ham slice a dressy look.

1	3½- to 4½-pound ham slice, (fully-cooked) 2- to 2½-inches thick	*Pineapple Topping*	
		1	can (1-pound 5-ounces) pineapple pie filling
Cherry Topping		3	tablespoons brown sugar
1	can (1-pound 5-ounces) cherry pie filling	2	teaspoons lemon juice
		¼	teaspoon curry
1	tablespoon lemon juice	½	cup raisins
1	teaspoon cinnamon		

Combine all ingredients for Cherry Topping or Pineapple Topping and mix well. Spoon topping on ham slice and place on smoker grid to smoke. Heat and serve extra topping with ham slices.

Charcoal: Use 5 pounds charcoal, 3 quarts hot water, 2 wood sticks and smoke 2 — 2½ hours.
Electric: Use 3 quarts hot water, 2 wood sticks and smoke 1½ — 2 hours.

Smoked Fresh Ham

Yield: 25 - 30 servings

Smoked fresh ham might be a welcome change from the cured ham that finds its way to the buffet supper and cocktail tables too many times.

1	16- to 18-pound fresh ham	1	cup consommé
1	cup brown sugar	1	teaspoon mustard seed
1	cup maple syrup	½	teaspoon celery seed
1	cup wine vinegar	½	teaspoon cracked pepper

Score ham about ½-inch deep across the top several times with a sharp knife. Combine other ingredients in a saucepan and bring to a boil. Pour mixture over ham and let ham stand overnight in refrigerator. Baste ham thoroughly with mixture then place on smoker grid. Baste with mixture 2 to 3 times during smoking and at the end of smoking. Cook remaining liquid down to a thick sauce and serve with ham. Meat thermometer should reach 185°F. for well done.

Charcoal: Use 15 pounds charcoal, 6 — 7 quarts hot water, 5 wood sticks (see note below) and smoke 6 — 8 hours.

Electric: Use 4 quarts hot water (may need to add water after 5 hours), 5 wood sticks (see note below) and smoke 5½ — 7½ hours.

Note: Start with 3 wood sticks and add 2 sticks after 3 hours of smoking.

Canadian Bacon

This is a quickie since the meat is already fully cooked. A nice dish to serve at a buffet.

	Canadian bacon, unsliced	Brown sugar
1	jar (8 ounces) apple jelly	2 ounces rum

Make slices in bacon an inch apart being careful not to slice completely through. Place bacon on tray constructed of 2 thicknesses of heavy-duty foil. Mix apple jelly and rum; spoon between slices and on top. Sprinkle with brown sugar and place bacon on foil tray in smoker.

Charcoal: Use 5 pounds charcoal, 3 quarts hot water, 2 wood sticks and smoke 30 minutes per pound.

Electric: Use 2 quarts hot water, 2 wood sticks and smoke 30 minutes per pound.

Mrs. Cook's Ham Loaf

Yield: 6 servings

A special family recipe acquired from a special friend and adapted for the water-smoker.

1	pound ground ham	*Sauce*	
1	pound fresh pork	1	cup brown sugar,
1	cup bread or cracker		firmly packed
	crumbs	½	teaspoon dry mustard
1	egg, beaten	¼	cup vinegar
½	cup evaporated milk	½	cup water

Mix thoroughly all ingredients, except sauce, and shape into a loaf that will fit in an 8″ square pan. Place loaf in pan and combine ingredients for sauce. Pour half of sauce over loaf and place pan, uncovered with loaf, on smoker grid. Pour remainder of sauce over loaf after 1 hour cooking. Spoon sauce over loaf after cooking and just before serving.

Charcoal: Use 5 pounds charcoal, 3 quarts hot water, 2 wood sticks and smoke 2½ − 3½ hours.
Electric: Use 3 quarts hot water, 2 wood sticks and smoke 2½ − 3 hours.

Fresh Pork Paté

Yield: 4 servings

Serve as an appetizer or main dish. This loaf is mild flavored and could be served with the Sweet Sauce recipe in the Sauces and Seasonings section.

1	pound ground lean fresh pork	2	hard cooked eggs, chopped
1	small onion, finely chopped		Pinch mace
		2	eggs, beaten
2	cups bread crumbs		Salt and pepper
		4	slices bacon

Combine pork, onion, bread crumbs, hard cooked eggs and mace. Stir in beaten eggs to bind the mixture and season. Form mixture in a loaf and wrap with bacon slices; two slices wrapped around loaf lengthwise and secured, two slices wrapped around the width and secured. The bacon slices help hold the shape of the loaf as well as add flavor. Place loaf on smoker grid and smoke.

Charcoal: Use 5 pounds charcoal, 3 quarts hot water, 1 wood stick and smoke 2½ − 3½ hours.
Electric: Use 3 quarts hot water, 1 wood stick and smoke 2 − 3 hours.

Poultry

Smoking poultry is a delight. The meat seems to absorb more of the smoke flavor. Served the next day, or cold, enhances the smoke flavor. We have prepared a wide variety of poultry recipes for your enjoyment. For whole chickens there is Italian Teriyaki, Chicken Intrigue and stuffed chicken recipes. Jamaican, Hawaiian, Caribbean, Smoker Chicken Casserole and Chicken Burgers are recipes using chicken pieces. Since Smoked Turkey is a favorite we have included a large variety of turkey recipes. It is certain you will find a favorite.

Honey-Glazed Turkey

Yield: 14 - 16 servings

Honey and butter brushed on the turkey makes it a beautiful golden brown and enhances the flavor.

1	14- to 16-pound turkey	½	cup wine
¼	cup melted butter or margarine	½	cup honey
		¼	teaspoon cinnamon

Wash turkey, remove giblets and neck and pat dry. Melt butter, remove from heat and stir in wine, honey and cinnamon. Cut several small slits in meat and inject ½ of mixture into meat with a baster or use a large syringe. Brush remaining ½ of mixture over turkey. If mixture is not injected, brush all of mixture on turkey and baste with mixture twice during cooking. Insert a meat thermometer for determining doneness and place turkey on smoker grid to water-smoke.

Charcoal: Use 15 pounds charcoal, 8 quarts hot water, 3 — 4 wood sticks and smoke 6 — 8 hours.

Electric: Use 4 quarts hot water, 3 — 4 wood sticks and smoke 6 — 8 hours.

Note: Add hot water to water pan in electric water-smoker after about 4 hours or as needed.

Smoked Whole Turkey

Yield: 11 - 13 servings

When served cold the next day, the smoked flavor of this meat is much stronger. Try Horseradish Sauce as a condiment.

1	11- to 13-pound turkey	3-4	ribs celery, chopped
1	stick butter or margarine, melted	1	medium onion, chopped
	Salt and pepper	1	large bay leaf, crumbled

Rinse turkey and pat dry. Rub inside of turkey generously with butter, salt and pepper. Stuff turkey with celery, onion and bay leaf. Place turkey on smoker grid and use a full water pan, adding water when needed.

Charcoal: Use 12 pounds charcoal, 6 quarts hot water, 3 wood sticks and smoke 6 — 7½ hours.

Electric: Use 4 quarts hot water, 3 wood sticks and smoke 5 — 7 hours.

Note: Add water to water pan in electric water — smoker after about 4 hours or as needed. Horseradish Sauce in Sauces section.

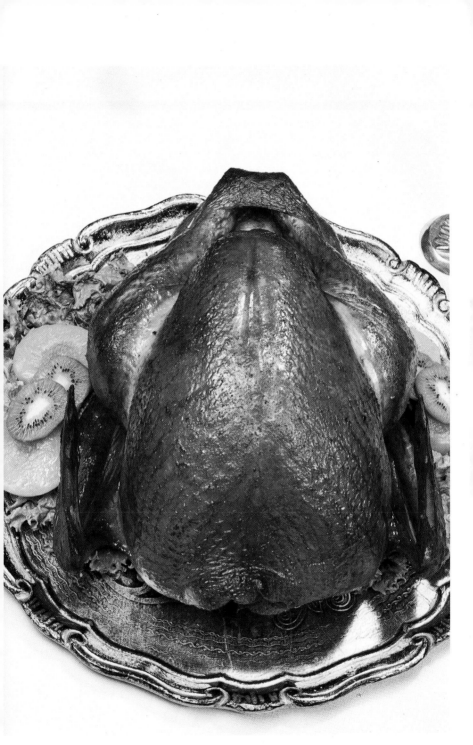

Honey Glazed Turkey

Drambuie Turkey

Yield: 14 - 16 servings

A favorite liqueur, Drambuie, gives turkey a sweet robust flavor. Try mesquite or fruit wood for smoking, although hickory is just fine. For more concentrated flavor from sauce, cut small slits in meat in several places and inject Drambuie sauce with a baster or use a large syringe. You can purchase one of good size from a veterinarian.

1 14- to 16-pound turkey	½ cup maple syrup
½ cup melted butter or margarine	¼ cup Drambuie

Remove giblets and neck. Wash turkey and pat dry. Mix melted butter, maple syrup and Drambuie. For more flavor from Drambuie mixture, cut several small slits in meat and inject ½ mixture with a baster or use a large syringe — one large enough to pass the thick mixture. A large syringe can be purchased from a veterinarian. Brush remaining ½ of mixture over turkey. If mixture is not injected brush all sauce over turkey and in cavity. Insert meat thermometer for determining doneness and place turkey on smoker grid to water-smoke. Brush again with mixture after cooking and while turkey is still hot.

Charcoal: Use 15 pounds charcoal, 8 quarts hot water, 3 — 4 wood sticks and smoke 6 — 8 hours.

Electric: Use 4 quarts hot water, 3 — 4 wood sticks and smoke 6 — 8 hours.

Note: Add hot water to water pan in electric water-smoker after 4 hours or as needed.

Smoked whole turkey is a holiday favorite, but also a great idea when turkeys are at a bargain price. Smoke more than one turkey and freeze extras for future meals. Wrap foil around leg ends and wing tips to prevent over-browning.

Ultimate Smoked Turkey

Yield: 8 - 10 servings

For gift giving or just pleasing your family, nothing beats a smoked turkey (executives call it the "ultimate gift"). The Super Smoking Sauce adds a super flavor.

1	8- to 10-pound turkey	½	cup white wine
1	medium onion	1	recipe of Super Smoking
2	bay leaves		Sauce (see note below)

Rinse turkey, pat dry and rub liberally with oil. Place onion, bay leaves and wine in water pan with hot water. Place water pan in smoker and turkey on smoker grid. Place dome on smoker and do not remove until midway through cooking time. Then remove dome and liberally paint turkey with Super Smoking Sauce. Replace dome and continue smoking. When turkey is done liberally paint again and allow to smoke for 15 minutes more.

Charcoal: Use 10 pounds charcoal, 5 quarts hot water, 3 wood sticks and smoke 4 – 6 hours.
Electric: Use 4 quarts hot water, 3 wood sticks and smoke 4 – 6 hours.
Note: Super Smoking Sauce recipe is in Sauces section.
  Add water to water pan after about 4 hours or as needed.

Stuffed Turkey Breast

Yield: 8 servings

For an easy to prepare special family meal use a prepared stuffing mix. There are many flavor varieties available and they are so quick to prepare.

1	4- to 5-pound turkey breast, bone in	½	cup CranOrange Cranberry Orange
1	box (6 ounces) prepared bread stuffing mix with herb butter and wild rice		Sauce

Rinse turkey breast, pat dry and set aside. Prepare bread stuffing mix according to package instructions. Cool mix, then stuff breast cavity and tie with string to hold stuffing in place. Place turkey breast on smoker grid and brush with CranOrange sauce. Use fruit wood for smoking if available.

Charcoal: Use 7 pounds charcoal, 4 quarts hot water, 2 wood sticks and smoke 3 – 4 hours.
Electric: Use 4 quarts hot water, 2 wood sticks and smoke 2½ – 3½ hours.
Note: Add hot water to water pan when needed.

Soy Turkey Breast

Yield: 10 - 12 servings

Delicious hot or cold — great in a Hawaiian turkey salad with pineapple.

1	5- to 6-pound turkey breast, bone-in	¼	cup oil
		1	tablespoon ginger
¼	cup soy sauce	1	tablespoon dry mustard
½	cup sherry	1	teaspoon garlic powder
¼	cup honey	½	teaspoon grated onion

Rinse turkey and pat dry. Combine remaining ingredients. Place turkey breast in a deep bowl or plastic bag. Pour sauce over turkey and marinate overnight, turning several times. Remove turkey from marinade and place on smoker grid. Baste turkey breast with sauce every 2 hours. When turkey is done, liberally brush again with sauce. For a stronger, smoked flavor, serve on the second day.

Charcoal: Use 7 — 8 pounds charcoal, 5 quarts hot water, 3 wood sticks and smoke 3½ — 4½ hours.

Electric: Use 4 quarts hot water, 3 wood sticks and smoke 3 — 4 hours.

Note: Add hot water to water pan when needed.

Honey-Glazed Breast of Turkey

Yield: 8 servings

Turkey breast is more expensive per pound but there is less waste and if your family prefers white meat it is the best buy.

1	4- to 5-pound turkey breast, bone-in	1	tablespoon butter or margarine
½	cup honey		Juice from ½ lemon
¼	cup dry sherry	½	teaspoon salt

Rinse turkey breast and pat dry. Heat honey, sherry and butter in a saucepan. Remove from heat, stir in lemon juice and salt. Pour honey mixture over turkey breast and let stand, covered, in refrigerator for 3-5 hours. Place turkey breast on smoker grid and baste. Baste once again when almost done.

Charcoal: Use 7 pounds charcoal, 4 quarts hot water, 2 wood sticks and smoke 3 — 4 hours.

Electric: Use 4 quarts hot water, 2 wood sticks, and smoke 2½ — 3½ hours.

Note: Add hot water to water pan when needed.

Turkey Roast

Yield: 12 - 14 servings

This is simply a boneless turkey and there is no waste.

1	4-pound turkey roast (boneless, rolled)	1	tablespoon grated orange peel
1	cup chili sauce	⅓	cup brown sugar
½	cup jellied cranberry sauce	1	teaspoon salt
		1	teaspoon dry mustard
½	cup cranberry juice	½	teaspoon ginger
2	tablespoons Worcestershire sauce	¼	teaspoon cayenne

Place turkey roast in an oblong dish. Combine remaining ingredients in a saucepan and heat until mixture is well blended. Cool and pour sauce over turkey roast, cover, and let stand in sauce in refrigerator 3 to 4 hours or overnight. Remove roast from sauce and place on smoker grid. Brush roast with sauce and brush once during smoking. When roast is cooked, heat sauce and serve with roast slices.

Charcoal: Use 8 pounds charcoal, 5 quarts hot water, 2 — 3 wood sticks and smoke 4 — 5 hours.
Electric: Use 4 quarts hot water, 2 — 3 wood sticks and smoke 4 — 4½ hours.
Note: Add hot water to water pan when needed.

Oriental Turkey Legs

Yield: 6 - 8 servings

A great way to use economically priced turkey legs.

4 - 6	turkey legs	½	cup soy sauce
1	envelope onion soup mix	½	teaspoon garlic powder
		2	teaspoons fresh ginger root, grated
½	cup oil		
1	cup cider vinegar	1	tablespoon sesame seeds

Rinse turkey legs, pat dry and place in a shallow dish or heavy-duty plastic bag. Combine all the remaining ingredients, except the sesame seeds, and pour over the turkey. Cover dish or close the bag securely and refrigerate overnight, turning the legs occasionally. Remove the turkey legs from the marinade and place on smoker grid. Pour marinade over turkey legs and into water pan. Sprinkle the legs with the sesame seeds and water-smoke.

Charcoal: Use 7 pounds charcoal, 4 quarts hot water, 3 wood sticks and smoke 2½ — 3½ hours.
Electric: Use 4 quarts hot water, 3 wood sticks and smoke 2 — 3 hours.

Turkey Wings With Dressing

Yield: 6 servings

There is surprisingly generous amounts of meat on a turkey wing — a terrific budget stretcher.

4 turkey wings, about 1 pound each	½ cup chopped celery
3 cups dressing	12 slices dry bread
Dressing	1 teaspoon salt
½ pound ground chuck or pork sausage	1 teaspoon poultry seasoning
½ cup chopped onion	2 eggs

Rinse turkey wings and pat dry. For the dressing, sauté the meat, onion and celery just until the meat starts to turn gray in color. Pour this mixture over bread, which has been soaked in water and pressed out. Add the seasonings and egg; then mix well. Assemble the turkey wings with the dressing as follows: put two wings outer side down, and place half dressing on each wing. Place remaining wings on top. Arrange wings on smoker grid and water-smoke. After smoking, slice turkey wings with a carving knife parallel to the bone, through both wings and dressing.

Charcoal: Use 7 pounds charcoal, 4 quarts hot water, 2 wood sticks and smoke 2½ — 3½ hours.
Electric: Use 4 quarts hot water, 2 wood sticks and smoke 2 — 3 hours.

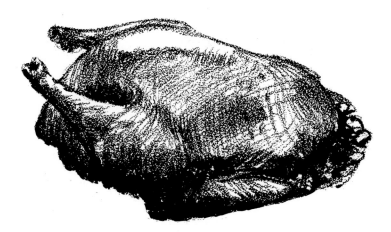

Tarragon Chicken

Yield: 4 servings

My favorite smoked food is smoked poultry. It is so moist and flavorful when water-smoked. Try this simple recipe as is or use white wine or fruit juice in water pan and see if you agree — smoked poultry is the best.

1 3- to 4-pound whole chicken	1 teaspoon dried tarragon
Peanut oil (or vegetable oil)	Garlic salt
1 tablespoon lemon juice	Seasoned pepper

Rinse chicken, pat dry and rub with oil. Combine lemon juice with tarragon and rub into cavity of chicken. Sprinkle outside with garlic salt and seasoned pepper. Place chicken on smoker grid and water-smoke.

Charcoal: Use 5 pounds charcoal, 3 quarts hot water, 2 wood sticks and smoke 2½ – 3 hours.
Electric: Use 3 quarts hot water, 2 wood sticks and smoke 2 – 2½ hours.

Italian Chicken

Yield: 4 servings

Italian dressing mix is the basic ingredient in this marinated chicken recipe. The longer it marinates the spunkier the flavor.

1 3- to 4-pound whole chicken	¼ cup white wine or lemon juice
1 package Italian dressing mix	1 tablespoon dried dill weed
½ cup vegetable oil	

Rinse chicken and pat dry. Combine remaining ingredients in a jar and shake until well mixed. Place chicken in a heavy-duty plastic bag with lock-seal, pour Italian marinade over chicken and seal bag. Coat chicken thoroughly and marinate overnight turning occasionally to coat entire chicken well. Remove from marinade (pour remaining marinade in water pan) and place on smoker grid to smoke.

Charcoal: Use 5 pounds charcoal, 3 quarts hot water, 2 wood sticks and smoke 2½ – 3 hours.
Electric: Use 3 quarts hot water, 2 wood sticks and smoke 2 – 2½ hours.

Smoked Chicken Teriyaki

Yield: 4 servings

Dress up plain chicken with this teriyaki sauce. The chicken is moist, with a very definite Oriental flavor.

1	3-pound whole chicken	½	teaspoon garlic powder
⅓	cup soy sauce	1½	teaspoons ginger
¼	cup sherry	1½	teaspoons dry mustard

Rinse chicken and pat dry. Place chicken in a large bowl or heavy-duty plastic bag. Combine all remaining ingredients in a small bowl and blend. Pour marinade into and over chicken. Turn chicken so the marinade coats it completely. Cover with plastic wrap or close bag securely. Refrigerate overnight, occasionally turning the chicken to thoroughly coat. Remove chicken from marinade and place on smoker grid. Pour marinade over chicken and let it drip into the water pan.

Charcoal: Use 5 pounds charcoal, 3 quarts hot water, 2 wood sticks and smoke 2½ − 3 hours.
Electric: Use 3 quarts hot water, 2 wood sticks and smoke 2 − 2½ hours.

Chicken Intrigue

Yield: 4 - 6 servings

A little unusual, but very good. When chickens are on special at the market, stock up to water-smoke.

2	2- to 3-pound whole chickens	1	teaspoon paprika
		1	teaspoon celery salt
1	cup mayonnaise	½	teaspoon sugar
3	ounces dry sherry	2	tablespoons Worcestershire sauce
2	tablespoons red wine vinegar		
		2	tablespoons bottled steak sauce
1	clove garlic, minced		
1	tablespoon Dijon mustard	¼	teaspoon red pepper sauce

Cut chickens in half, rinse and pat dry. Combine all ingredients, except chickens, and mix well. Brush marinade over chicken several hours before cooking or marinate overnight in refrigerator. Place chicken halves on smoker grid and brush once again with sauce. Brush once again with sauce during cooking. Smoke according to directions below.

Charcoal: Use 5 pounds charcoal, 3 quarts hot water, 2 wood sticks and smoke 2½ − 3½ hours.
Electric: Use 3 quarts hot water, 2 wood sticks and smoke 2 − 3 hours.

Tomato Chicken

Yield: 4 - 6 servings

The combination of ingredients is the secret to the tasty flavor of this sauce for chicken.

2	2- to 3-pound whole chickens	1	clove garlic, minced
1	can (15 ounce) tomato sauce	2	tablespoons sugar
¼	cup Worchestershire sauce	1	teaspoon dry mustard
1	onion, finely chopped	1	tablespoon parsley
		1	teaspoon thyme
		¼	cup red wine

Rinse chickens and place in a glass dish or 2 heavy-duty plastic bags. Combine remaining ingredients and pour over chickens. Cover dish or seal bags and marinate 2 hours or overnight. Remove chickens from dish or bags and place on smoker grid. Pour some of sauce on chickens and save remainder to heat and serve with chickens.

Charcoal: Use 5 pounds charcoal, 3 quarts hot water, 2—3 wood sticks and smoke 2½ — 3½ hours.
Electric: Use 3 quarts hot water, 2—3 wood sticks and smoke 2—3 hours.

Chicken, high in protein and B vitamins, is low calorie and economical. Chickens vary in size — a small 2-3 pounds serves two and a larger 4-5 pounds serves five to six people.

Smoked Whole Chicken

Yield: 4 servings

Moist and tender — no sauces needed. This is delicious cold, so smoke several at one time.

1	3- to 4-pound whole chicken	1	rib celery, with tops
	Salt (optional)	2	slices onion
		1	small bay leaf

Rinse chicken inside and out and blot dry. Rub cavity lightly with salt, if you wish. Place the celery, onion, and bay leaf in cavity. Place chicken on smoker grid and smoke.

Charcoal: Use 5 pounds charcoal, 3 quarts hot water, 2 wood sticks and smoke 2½ — 3 hours.
Electric: Use 3 quarts hot water, 2 wood sticks and smoke 2 — 2½ hours.

Seasoned Chickens

Yield: 8 - 10 servings

Cooking for a crowd? Try economical, juicy Seasoned Chickens. Keep the heat and mess out of the kitchen.

   4   2- to 3-pound chickens
Vegetable oil
Seasoned salt

Rinse chickens and pat dry. Rub with oil and sprinkle thoroughly with seasoned salt. Place 2 chickens on top grid and 2 on bottom grid. For extra flavor use half water and half apple cider (heat cider to speed cooking).

Charcoal: Use 8 — 10 pounds charcoal, 4 quarts hot water, 3 wood sticks, and smoke 3 — 4 hours.
Electric: Use 4 quarts hot water, 3 wood sticks and smoke 2½ — 3½ hours.

Chicken With Wild Pecan Rice Stuffing

Yield: 5 - 6 servings

Try something special, Wild Pecan Rice Stuffing instead of regular wild rice. Of course wild rice could also be used.

1 5-pound whole chicken	¼ cup canned mushrooms, chopped
½ cup Wild Pecan Rice	1 can (8¼ ounces) crushed pineapple, drained
1 tablespoon instant chicken bouillon	¼ cup chopped cashews or peanuts
½ pound sausage	1 tablespoon dried parsley
¼ cup chopped onion	Dash nutmeg
¼ cup chopped celery	Dash dry mustard
¼ cup chopped green pepper	1 egg, beaten

Rinse, pat dry and season chicken with salt and pepper. Meanwhile cook rice according to package instructions adding bouillon to water. Do not over cook rice. As the rice cooks, brown sausage in a large skillet. Add onions, celery and green pepper and cook until soft. Stir in remaining ingredients in the order given, including rice. Cool slightly and stuff chicken cavity loosely, then secure opening.

Charcoal: Use 7 pounds charcoal, 3 quarts hot water, 2 wood sticks and smoke 3 — 3½ hours.
Electric: Use 3 quarts hot water, 2 wood sticks and smoke 2½ — 3 hours.

Chicken With Cornbread-Walnut Stuffing

Yield: 5 - 6 servings

Don't wait until Thanksgiving to enjoy that stuffed fowl. The water-smoker can be used all year long.

1	5-pound roasting whole chicken	1	teaspoon salt
½	cup chopped green onions	¼	teaspoon pepper
½	cup chopped celery	¼	teaspoon thyme
¼	cup butter or margarine	½	teaspoon poultry seasoning
2	cups cornbread stuffing		Dash sage (optional)
1	cup toasted white bread cubes	¼	cup milk or chicken broth
1	cup chopped walnuts	2	eggs, beaten

Rinse chicken and pat dry. Sauté onion and celery in butter for 5 minutes. Combine stuffing, bread cubes, walnuts, and seasonings in a large bowl. Add eggs and milk and toss. Fill chicken loosely with stuffing and secure openings. Sprinkle chicken with seasoned salt and place on smoker grid. Smoke as instructed below.

Charcoal: Use 7 pounds charcoal, 3 quarts hot water, 2 wood sticks and smoke 3 — 3½ hours.
Electric: Use 3 quarts hot water, 2 wood sticks and smoke 2½ — 3 hours.

Herbed Chickens

Yield: 8 - 10 servings

A good recipe for chicken bargain days. Cook a lot, freeze for later.

4	2- to 3-pound chickens	½	teaspoon each of thyme, basil, chili powder, oregano, dry mustard, cloves and salt
1	pound butter or margarine, melted		
	Juice of 3 lemons		
1	tablespoon tarragon vinegar	2	cloves of garlic, minced
1	tablespoon sugar		

Rinse chicken inside and outside. Pat dry and place in marinade dish or in heavy-duty plastic bags. Combine all remaining ingredients and pour over chickens. Cover or seal bags and marinate for 24 hours. Remove chickens from marinade and place on smoker grids. Pour remaining marinade over chickens and let it drip into water pan.

Charcoal: Use 8 — 10 pounds charcoal, 4 quarts hot water, 3 wood sticks and smoke 3 — 4 hours.
Electric: Use 4 quarts hot water, 3 wood sticks and smoke 2½ — 3½ hours.

Caribbean Chicken

Yield: 4 - 6 servings

Frozen limeade is used for a tart but sweet flavor. This marinade is complimented by the addition of bubbling ginger ale.

2	2- to 3-pound chickens, cut in halves or quartered	1	tablespoon minced onion
1	can (6 ounces) frozen limeade concentrate, thawed	½	cup honey
		1	teaspoon tarragon
			Dash pepper
⅓	cup vegetable oil	½	cup ginger ale

Rinse chicken and pat dry. Put chicken pieces in a large heavy-duty plastic bag or shallow non-aluminum container. Combine remaining ingredients and pour over chicken. Marinate in the refrigerator overnight. Remove chicken from marinade and place on smoker grid. Pour remaining marinade into smoker water pan and prepare smoker.

Charcoal: Use 5 — 7 pounds charcoal, 3 quarts hot water, 2 wood sticks and smoke 2½ — 3 hours.
Electric: Use 3 quarts hot water, 2 wood sticks and smoke 2 — 2½ hours.

Jamaican Chicken

Yield: 4 - 6 servings

A spicy sauce gives chicken a special out-of-this-world flavor.

2	2½-pound chickens, split	1	tablespoon Worcestershire sauce
½	cup chili sauce	½	teaspoon dry mustard
2	tablespoons cider vinegar	½	cup minced onion
1	teaspoon salt	1	clove garlic, minced
½	teaspoon pepper	2	tablespoons vegetable oil

Wash and dry chickens. Combine the remaining ingredients in a bowl and marinate chickens for 3 - 4 hours in this mixture. Remove chickens from marinade and place on smoker grid. Brush with marinade sauce before cooking and just before serving.

Charcoal: Use 5 pounds charcoal, 3 quarts hot water, 2 wood sticks and smoke 2½ — 3 hours.
Electric: Use 3 quarts hot water, 2 wood sticks and smoke 2 — 2½ hours.

Hawaiian Chicken

Yield: 4 - 6 servings

A superb combination of chicken, pineapple and coconut gives this recipe a tropical flavor.

2 2½-pound chickens, split	¼ cup finely chopped green pepper
1 can (8 ounces) crushed pineapple	1 tablespoon oil
¼ cup pineapple juice	1 tablespoon lime juice
1 cup grated or flaked coconut	¼ cup honey

Rinse and pat dry chickens. Drain pineapple reserving ¼ cup of juice. Combine pineapple, pineapple juice and remaining ingredients. Place chickens on smoker grid and top with pineapple-coconut mixture. Save remaining topping. Smoke according to instructions below. Spoon remaining topping on a platter and place broilers on top to serve. Garnish with lime peel or mint leaves.

Charcoal: Use 5 pounds charcoal, 3 quarts hot water, 2 wood sticks and smoke 2½ − 3 hours.
Electric: Use 3 quarts hot water, 2 wood sticks and smoke 2 − 2½ hours.

Cranberry Glazed Chicken

Yield: 4 servings

Nothing's better than poultry and cranberries. It is good any time, not just holidays. Although fresh cranberries are seasonal, canned jellied cranberries used in this recipe are available year around.

1 3- to 4-pound chicken, cut into serving pieces	1 tablespoon soy sauce
1 can (8 ounces) jellied cranberry sauce	¼ cup butter or margarine
¼ cup orange marmalade	Dash salt

Rinse chicken and pat dry. Mix remaining ingredients in a sauce pan and heat until well blended. Cool, and pour over chicken that has been placed in large shallow dish. Coat chicken well with sauce and marinate 5 - 6 hours or overnight in refrigerator. Remove chicken from sauce and place on smoker grid. Brush chicken with sauce before and while cooking. Save any remaining sauce to serve with chicken.

Charcoal: Use 5 pounds charcoal, 3 quarts hot water, 2 wood sticks and smoke 1½ − 2½ hours.
Electric: Use 3 quarts hot water, 2 wood sticks and smoke 1½ − 2½ hours.

Catalina Chicken

Yield: 4 servings

An easy sauce to make with a slightly sweet and tangy flavor. Bottled Catalina salad dressing makes it easy and flavorful.

1	3-pound chicken, cut into serving pieces	1	envelope onion soup mix
1	bottle (8 ounces) Catalina salad dressing	½	teaspoon poultry seasoning

Rinse chicken pieces and pat dry. Combine salad dressing, onion soup mix and poultry seasoning, mix well. Place chicken in heavy-duty plastic bag (or glass shallow dish) with salad dressing mixture and marinate 3 to 4 hours in refrigerator. Place chicken pieces on smoker grid and brush with sauce before and once during cooking. These chicken pieces can also be cooked in an uncovered heat resistant pan and covered with sauce. If cooked in a pan, eliminate marinating and increase smoking time about 30 minutes.

Charcoal: Use 5 pounds charcoal, 3 quarts hot water, 2 wood sticks and smoke 1½ – 2 hours.
Electric: Use 3 quarts hot water, 2 wood sticks and smoke 1½ – 2 hours.

Chicken in Spaghetti Sauce

Yield: 4 - 6 Servings

Dry spaghetti sauce mix becomes a delicious sauce as the chicken cooks. So easy you will want to keep the mix on hand for a quick meal.

2	2- to 3-pound chickens, cut into serving pieces	⅛	teaspoon garlic powder
½	cup vegetable oil		Salt and pepper
2	packages (1½ ounce) spaghetti sauce mix	¼	cup red wine (optional)

Rinse chicken and pat dry. Pour oil into a heat resistant large shallow pan. Roll chicken in oil thoroughly coating each piece. Combine spaghetti sauce, garlic powder, salt and pepper in a bowl or plastic bag. Place chicken pieces, 2 - 3 at a time, in spaghetti sauce mixture and thoroughly coat each. Place chicken fat sides up in pan with oil and pour in red wine. Place pan uncovered on smoker grid. Two small pans could be used placing one on top grid and one on bottom.

Charcoal: Use 5 – 7 pounds charcoal, 3 quarts hot water, 2 wood sticks and smoke 2 – 3 hours.
Electric: Use 3 quarts hot water, 2 wood sticks and smoke 2 – 3 hours.

**Tarragon Chicken, Catalina
Chicken Pieces**

Smoker Chicken Casserole

Yield: 4 - 6 servings

If your family enjoys casseroles here is a good one to fix on the smoker.

3	pounds chicken pieces	1	teaspoon salt
1	can (10 ounces) Golden Cream of Mushroom soup	¼	teaspoon pepper
		1	teaspoon red pepper flakes
1	can (10 ounces) Cream of Celery soup	½	cup slivered almonds
		¼	cup dry Vermouth
1	can (10 ounces) Cream of Chicken soup		Parmesan cheese

Rinse chicken pieces and place in the bottom of a greased 9" x 14" casserole or foil dish. Mix other ingredients, except cheese, in a large bowl and pour over chicken. Sprinkle with Parmesan cheese. Place dish uncovered on smoker grid and smoke. Serve with rice or noodles.

Charcoal: Use 5 pounds charcoal, 3 quarts hot water, 2 wood sticks and smoke 2 – 2½ hours.

Electric: Use 3 quarts hot water, 1 wood stick and smoke 2 – 2½ hours.

Chicken Burgers

Yield: 8 servings

Tired of hamburgers — try these delicious smoked chicken burgers. Smoke these along with ground meat patties and give your family a choice.

8	chicken thighs	¼	teaspoon tarragon
	Barbecue salt or salt	1	teaspoon lemon juice
2	tablespoons prepared mustard	8	seeded hamburger buns

Cut slits lengthwise in each thigh along bone. Cut meat away from bone; wash and pat dry. Sprinkle both sides lightly with barbecue salt or salt. Combine remaining ingredients except buns and brush on meat. Place meat on smoker grid and smoke. When meat is done spread butter on buns and toast. Serve with sliced tomatoes, onions, pickles and lettuce.

Charcoal: Use 5 pounds charcoal, 3 quarts hot water, 1 wood stick and smoke 1 – 1½ hours.

Electric: Use 2 quarts hot water, 1 wood stick and smoke 1 – 1½ hours.

Taco Chicken

Yield: 4 - 6 servings

Smoked, spicy chicken pieces are a great addition to a Mexican menu. For this recipe select any chicken parts that you prefer or that are on sale.

2- to 3-pounds chicken thighs, wings, quarters or legs
1 package (1½ ounces) taco seasoning mix

⅔ cup buttermilk biscuit mix

Rinse chicken pieces and pat dry. In a bowl, mix together taco seasoning and biscuit mix. Roll chicken pieces into dry mix until pieces are well coated. Place pieces on smoker grid and smoke.

Charcoal: Use 5 pounds charcoal, 3 quarts hot water, 1 wood stick and smoke 1 – 2 hours.
Electric: Use 3 quarts hot water, 1 wood stick and smoke 1 – 2 hours.

Poultry seems to absorb the smoke flavor more than other meats and the skin helps hold in the juices. The smoke flavor strengthens when poultry and other meats are refrigerated overnight.

Luau Drumsticks

Yield: 4 servings

Sweet and juicy!

8 chicken legs
1 jar (8 ounces) peach or apricot preserves
¼ cup lemon juice
¼ cup vegetable oil

¼ cup molasses
2 tablespoons soy sauce
½ teaspoon salt
¼ teaspoon pepper
½ teaspoon ginger

Rinse chicken legs and pat dry. Combine remaining ingredients and mix well. Place chicken legs in a large shallow dish and pour on sauce. Let legs set in sauce 2 - 3 hours turning occasionally. Remove legs from sauce and place on smoker grid. Brush with sauce before smoking, once during smoking and just before serving.

Charcoal: Use 5 pounds charcoal, 3 quarts hot water, 1 wood stick and smoke 1½ – 2 hours.
Electric: Use 2 quarts hot water, 1 wood stick and smoke 1½ – 2 hours.

Sweet and Hot Drumsticks

Yield: 6 servings

Smoke a lot at one time and freeze. Quick to thaw and heat in the microwave.

12	chicken legs	Tarragon
1	cup sweet and hot mustard	Bacon
		Salt and pepper

Rinse chicken legs and pat dry. Thoroughly spread mustard on each chicken leg coating well. Sprinkle with tarragon and wrap each leg with a bacon slice. Secure bacon with a toothpick and season legs with salt and pepper. Place legs on smoker grid and smoke.

Charcoal: Use 5 pounds charcoal, 3 quarts hot water, 2 wood sticks and smoke 1½ − 2 hours.
Electric: Use 3 quarts hot water, 2 wood sticks and smoke 1½ − 2 hours.

Pizza Wings

Yield: 4 servings, 6 - 8 servings as an appetizer

No sauce could be simpler — all you need is bottled (or canned) pizza sauce, a little wine and fennel seeds if you desire.

12	chicken wings (approx. 3 pounds)	¼	cup red wine
2	cups pizza sauce	2	teaspoons fennel seeds (optional)

Rinse chicken wings and pat dry. Lock wing tips so they will be more compact. Combine remaining ingredients and pour over wings. Let set 2 to 3 hours in refrigerator and then place wings on smoker grid. Brush wings with sauce before smoking. Brush with sauce once again after cooking.

Charcoal: Use 5 pounds charcoal, 3 quarts hot water, 1 wood stick and smoke 1 − 1½ hours.
Electric: Use 2 quarts hot water, 1 wood stick and smoke 1 − 1½ hours.

Sausage Stuffed Chicken Breasts

Yield: 8 servings

The sausage stuffing gives a delightful flavor to the smoked chicken breast.

4 whole chicken breasts, skinned, split and boned	½ cup chopped green onion
	½ cup melted butter or margarine
8 pre-cooked breakfast link sausages	Paprika, salt, pepper
	Parsley

Pound chicken breast halves to flatten. Place one sausage at end of each half, add a few onions and roll up breasts. Secure with string, small skewers or toothpicks. Brush each breast-half with melted butter and season with paprika, salt and pepper. Top each with a pinch of parsley and place on smoker grid. Smoke according to directions below.

Charcoal: Use 5 pounds charcoal, 3 quarts hot water, 1 wood stick and smoke 1 — 1½ hours.

Electric: Use 2 quarts hot water, 1 wood stick and smoke 1 — 1½ hours.

Glazed Chicken Breast

Yield: 4 servings

A delicious peachy glaze with a hint of rum.

2 whole chicken breasts, split	1 teaspoon lemon-pepper
¾ cup peach preserves	2 tablespoons steak sauce
¼ cup rum	1 tablespoon toasted sesame seeds

Rinse and pat dry chicken breast. In a bowl, combine remaining ingredients except sesame seeds. Toast sesame seeds at a low temperature in the oven. Place chicken breast in peach glaze and marinate 2 - 3 hours. Remove chicken and place on smoker grid and top with peach glaze mixture. Sprinkle sesame seeds on top of each chicken piece and smoke.

Charcoal: Use 5 pounds charcoal, 3 quarts hot water, 1 — 2 wood sticks and smoke 1½ — 2 hours.

Electric: Use 3 quarts hot water, 1 — 2 wood sticks and smoke 1½ — 2 hours.

Smoker-Baked Chicken Breast

Yield: 4 servings

A simple recipe for last-minute fixing.

4 whole chicken breasts	Salt
Juice of 1 lemon	Seasoned pepper
¼ cup butter or margarine	6 slices of onion

Rinse chicken breast and pat dry. Place chicken in a shallow baking dish or pan. Sprinkle with lemon juice and place a pat of butter on top of each breast. Sprinkle with salt and seasoned pepper, then top with sliced onions. Place chicken breast directly on smoker grid and smoke.

Charcoal: Use 5 pounds charcoal, 3 quarts hot water, 1 – 2 wood sticks and smoke 1½ – 2 hours.
Electric: Use 3 quarts hot water, 1 – 2 wood sticks and smoke 1½ – 2 hours.

Chili Cheese Roll-Ups

Yield: 4 servings

This recipe is worth the extra work of boning the chicken breast.

2 whole chicken breasts, skinned, split and boned	⅓ cup chopped green chilies
¾ to 1 cup grated Monterey Jack cheese	½ cup bread crumbs
Cumin powder	½ teaspoon chili powder
	Oil

Pound chicken breast halves to flatten. Top each with grated cheese and chilies. Season lightly with cumin powder. Roll up breast halves and secure with string, small skewers or toothpicks. Brush lightly with oil and roll in a mixture of bread crumbs with chili powder. Place roll-ups on smoker grid and water-smoke.

Charcoal: Use 5 pounds charcoal, 3 quarts hot water, 1 wood stick and smoke 1 – 1½ hours.
Electric: Use 2 quarts hot water, 1 wood stick and smoke 1 – 1½ hours.

Lamb & Veal

Lamb, a favorite of many, is irresistible when smoked. With the water smoker it is unlikely you will overcook. Smoked Leg of Lamb, Spiced Leg of Lamb, Mushroom Stuffed Lamb Chops and Dill Chops are a few of the water-smoked recipes you will want to try.

Veal also is very good smoked. Romano Veal Roast, Canadian Veal Roast, Crab Stuffed Veal Steaks and Veal Cheese Loaf are recipes we have selected to share.

Crown Roast of Lamb

Yield: 4 servings

Fit for a king! Something special for Father's Day. Serve with mint jelly.

1 small crown roast of lamb (about 3 pounds)	1 package (5 ounces) Wild Brown Rice with Mushrooms
Salt and pepper	2 cups boiling water
3-4 slices bacon	1 small can mandarin oranges
½ cup sliced leek or green onions	

Order crown roast from butcher a few days ahead of time, or buy a rack of lamb ribs and make the crown yourself. The butcher will usually supply the crown frills for the top of ribs. For a larger crown roast use 2 racks of lamb ribs and increase cooking time (increase charcoal and hot water accordingly).

Season crown roast lightly with salt and pepper and set aside. Fry bacon until crisp, remove from heat, drain and crumble. Sauté leek slices or green onion in bacon drippings until soft. Stir in rice and toss with drippings; add boiling water and seasoning mix. Bring mixture to a boil, lower heat and cover pan. Simmer until rice is tender and liquid is absorbed, about 4 — 5 minutes. Remove from heat and add crumbled bacon and ½ mandarin oranges. Toss lightly. Place roast in a foil pie pan or on a double thickness of heavy-duty foil. Fill crown roast with rice mixture. Place a piece of foil over top of roast, just to cover top. This will keep rice and rib tops from over browning. Place roast on smoker grid and water-smoke. After cooked, let rest on warm platter about 15 minutes. Decorate ribs with crown frills and garnish with leaf lettuce and remainder of mandarin oranges. Carve between ribs and serve with rice stuffing.

Charcoal: Use 7 pounds charcoal, 4 quarts hot water, 2 wood sticks and smoke 2 — 2½ hours.
Electric: Use 3 quarts hot water, 2 wood sticks and smoke 1½ - 2 hours.

**Crown Roast of Lamb and
Smoked Leg of Lamb**

Barbecued Leg of Lamb

Yield: 8 servings

Barbecue sauce and beer give leg of lamb a special flavor. This is really a simple recipe.

1	5- to 6-pound leg of lamb	1	can beer (12 ounces)
2	cloves garlic	2	tablespoons Worcestershire sauce
1	bottle barbecue sauce	2-3	drops red pepper sauce
		1	teaspoon salt

Trim fat on roast to ⅛ inch. Cut 4 deep slits in roast. Slice each clove of garlic in half and place in slits. Place roast in deep bowl. Combine remaining ingredients and pour over roast, cover and place in refrigerator for 6-8 hours or overnight. Remove roast from sauce and place on smoker grid, brushing liberally with sauce. Brush again with sauce one hour before completion of smoking. Remove garlic before slicing to serve. Serve with heated sauce.

Charcoal: Use 8 pounds charcoal, 4 quarts hot water, 3 wood sticks and smoke 3½ — 4½ hours.
Electric: Use 4 quarts hot water, 3 wood sticks and smoke 3 — 4 hours.

Spiced Leg of Lamb

Yield: 8 servings

An unusual combination of spices gives this leg of lamb a distinct and delicious flavor.

1	5-pound leg of lamb	1	teaspoon curry
1	can (6 ounces) tomato paste	1	teaspoon cumin
½	cup beef stock	1	teaspoon paprika
3	tablespoons Vermouth	1	teaspoon salt
1	tablespoon vegetable oil	½	teaspoon ginger

Trim fat on lamb to ⅛ inch thick. In a bowl, combine remaining ingredients and mix well. Coat lamb with a thick layer of spice mixture and place on smoker grid. Use a meat thermometer to best determine doneness.

Charcoal: Use 8 pounds charcoal, 4 quarts hot water, 3 wood sticks and smoke 3½ — 4 hours.
Electric: Use 4 quarts hot water, 3 wood sticks and smoke 3 — 3½ hours.

Smoked Leg of Lamb

Yield: 8 servings

Garlicky and mildly seasoned, this Smoked Leg of Lamb will please all. If you desire, a barbecue sauce could be served with the sliced lamb.

1 5-pound leg of lamb	Seasoned salt
4-5 small cloves of garlic	Seasoned pepper
Fresh parsley	Rosemary
Peanut oil	Barbecue sauce (optional)
Gin (2 ounces)	

Trim fat on lamb to ⅛ inch. Make 4 deep holes in the top surface of lamb and insert 1 whole peeled garlic clove in each hole. Push a sprig of parsley in on top of garlic to indicate location so garlic can be removed when meat is done. Rub entire surface of meat with peanut oil and gin, then sprinkle with seasoned salt, seasoned ground black pepper, and rosemary. Let lamb stand at room temperature 30 minutes, then place on smoker grid and water-smoke. Use a meat thermometer to determine doneness. Remove garlic before serving. Let stand 10 minutes for meat to firm before carving. Serve with barbecue sauce if desired.

Charcoal: Use 8 pounds charcoal, 4 quarts hot water, 3 wood sticks and smoke
*   3½ − 4 hours.*
Electric: Use 4 quarts hot water, 3 wood sticks and smoke 3 − 3½ hours.

A Leg of Lamb is perfect for the water smoker. Slice and serve with barbecue sauce.

Marinated Lamb Shoulder

Yield: 8 servings

For those who enjoy leg of lamb, try this shoulder lamb roast. This cut is often less expensive but may have to be ordered from your butcher.

1	5- to 6-pound lamb shoulder roast	1	teaspoon parsley
½	cup lemon juice	½	teaspoon rosemary
¾	cup olive oil	½	teaspoon basil
2	teaspoons salt	1	clove garlic
1	tablespoon cracked black pepper	¾	cup chopped green onion or shallots
1	tablespoon Accent		Red pepper to taste
			Lemon Barbecue Sauce (see note)

Trim fat on roast and place in a deep bowl or heavy-duty plastic bag. Combine remaining ingredients and pour over lamb roast. Cover bowl or seal bag and marinate roast overnight. Remove roast, place on smoker grid and water-smoke. Serve with Lemon Barbecue Sauce.

Charcoal: Use 8 pound charcoal, 4 quarts hot water, 3 wood sticks and smoke 3½ − 4½ hours.
Electric: Use 4 quarts hot water, 3 wood sticks and smoke 3 − 4 hours.
Note: Lemon Barbecue Sauce in Sauces section.

Barbecued Lamb Chops

Yield: 6 servings

This apple-barbecue sauce would be just as good on lamb ribs or lamb shanks.

6	loin or rib lamb chops	⅔	cup catsup
2	apples, peeled and ground	¼	cup butter or margarine
1	medium onion, chopped	½	teaspoon salt
2	tablespoons chopped green pepper	¼	teaspoon pepper

Trim excess fat from chops. Combine remaining ingredients in a saucepan and boil 5 minutes. Cool sauce and spread liberally over chops. Place chops on smoker grid and brush with sauce. Brush chops with sauce after smoking and serve sauce hot with chops.

Charcoal: Use 5 pounds charcoal, 3 quarts hot water, 2 wood sticks and smoke 1 − 2 hours.
Electric: Use 3 quarts hot water, 2 wood sticks and smoke 1 − 2 hours.

Lamb Chops and Apples

Yield: 4 - 6 servings

These lamb chops, with a topping of apple pie filling, are cooked in a pan. So moist and juicy you will want to try these again.

4 large, loin lamb chops or 6 small chops	2 teaspoon pumpkin pie spice
Seasoned salt	⅓ cup apple or mint jelly
1 can apple pie filling	

Trim excess fat from chops and sprinkle with seasoned salt. Place chops in a heat-proof pan or foil pan. Combine remaining ingredients and pour over chops. Place pan on smoker grid and water-smoke.

Charcoal: Use 5 pounds charcoal, 3 quarts hot water, 2 wood sticks and smoke 1½ − 2 hours.
Electric: Use 3 quarts hot water, 2 wood sticks and smoke 1½ − 2 hours.

Pineapple Stuffed Lamb Chops

Yield: 4 servings

Fruit and lamb make an excellent duo. Stuff with as much pineapple as possible.

4 loin lamb chops, 1½ inch thick, with pocket	¼ teaspoon salt
Juice of 1 orange	Mint sprigs (if using apple or currant jelly)
1 tablespoon grated orange rind	¾ cup pineapple chunks
½ cup mint, currant or apple jelly	1 tablespoon sherry

Trim excess fat from chops. Combine remaining ingredients, except pineapple, in a saucepan and heat until jelly dissolves. Cool jelly sauce and stir in pineapple and sherry. Place chops in a shallow dish, pour sauce over chops and marinate 4-6 hours in refrigerator. Remove chops and pineapple chunks from sauce. Drain pineapple chunks well and stuff in pocket of chops. Brush chops with sauce and place on smoker grid. Heat sauce and serve with chops.

Charcoal: Use 5 pounds charcoal, 3 quarts hot water, 1 wood stick and smoke 1 − 2 hours.
Electric: Use 3 quarts hot water, 1 wood stick and smoke 1 − 2 hours.

Mushroom and Onion Stuffed Lamb Chops

Yield: 4 servings

These loin chops are mild in flavor. Even those who do not love lamb will appreciate the taste of these stuffed chops.

4	loin lamb chops, 1½ inch thick, with pocket	1	tablespoon oil
		1	cup sliced mushrooms
	Garlic salt	½	cup chopped onion
	Oregano	1	tablespoon parsley
	Rosemary	¼	cup bread crumbs
2	tablespoons butter or margarine	1	tablespoon Parmesan cheese

Season chops with garlic salt, oregano and rosemary. Sauté mushrooms and onion in butter and oil until soft. Remove from heat and stir in parsley, bread crumbs and cheese. Stuff each pocket with as much mushroom mixture as possible. Place chops on smoker grid and water-smoke.

Charcoal: Use 5 pounds charcoal, 3 quarts hot water, 2 wood sticks and smoke 1 – 2 hours.
Electric: Use 3 quarts hot water, 2 wood sticks and smoke 1 – 2 hours.

Dill Lamb Chops

Yield: 6 servings

A hint of dill in a sour cream marinade gives these chops a marvelous flavor.

6	loin lamb chops, 1 inch thick	1	tablespoon chopped chives
1	cup sour cream	½	teaspoon garlic salt
2	tablespoons wine vinegar	½	teaspoon salt
1	tablespoon dillweed	¼	teaspoon pepper

Trim excess fat from chops and place chops, one deep, in a glass shallow dish. In a glass bowl combine remaining ingredients. Coat both sides of chops with sour cream mixture, cover dish and marinate 3-4 hours in refrigerator. Remove from dish and place on smoker grid, coating with remainder of sour cream marinade. Serve with any remaining sour cream marinade.

Charcoal: Use 5 pounds charcoal, 3 quarts hot water, 1 wood stick and smoke 1 – 2 hours.
Electric: Use 3 quarts hot water, 1 wood stick and smoke 1 – 2 hours.

Romano Veal Roast

Yield: 4 - 6 servings

Veal has less fat than beef; therefore, the uncooked sausage stuffing adds seasoning and moistness to the veal as it cooks.

1 3- to 4-pound veal rump roast, boneless	1 can (8 ounces) tomato sauce
Salt and pepper	2 teaspoons Italian seasoning
1 pound pork sausage	1 teaspoon garlic powder
Fennel seeds (optional)	

Have the butcher bone a veal rump roast to weigh about 3-4 pounds, boneless. It will be tied so you will have to untie it to stuff, then tie again. After you have untied the roast, season with salt and pepper. The veal pieces will be unequal in size so select the larger piece for the bottom. Top the bottom half of the veal roast with uncooked sausage, spreading the sausage evenly, almost to the edges. Sprinkle the sausage with fennel seeds if desired. Place other veal half on top of sausage (top half may not completely cover sausage) and tie securely with string. Mix remaining ingredients for sauce and spread thickly over tied veal. Place veal on smoker grid and water-smoke.

Charcoal: Use 5 pounds charcoal, 3 quarts hot water, 2 wood sticks and smoke 1½ — 2½ hours.
Electric: Use 3 quarts hot water, 2 wood sticks and smoke 1½ — 2½ hours.
Note: For larger veal roast use 7 pounds charcoal.

A boneless rolled veal roast can be smoked without stuffing. Serve with a garnish of boiled onions filled with cream of peas with pearl onions.

Canadian Veal Roast

Yield: 4 - 6 servings

Canadian bacon and cheese is the simple stuffing for this veal roast.

1	3- to 4-pound veal rump roast, boneless	5-6	slices Canadian bacon
		3-4	slices mozzarella cheese
	Salt and pepper	3-4	regular bacon slices

Have your butcher bone a veal rump roast to weigh 3-4 pounds, boneless. Untie the boneless veal rump roast, season with salt and pepper. Place Canadian bacon slices on top of one half and top with cheese slices. Place other piece of roast on top of cheese. Trim excess Canadian bacon and cheese, then retie roast. Place uncooked regular bacon slices on top of roast for moistness. Place roast on smoker grid and water-smoke.

Charcoal: Use 5 pounds charcoal, 3 quarts hot water, 2 wood sticks and smoke 1½ − 2½ hours.
Electric: Use 3 quarts hot water, 2 wood sticks and smoke 1½ − 2½ hours.

Veal Cheese Loaf

Yield: 4 - 6 servings

You'll be amazed at how delicious and tasty this loaf is. It has a completely different flavor than beef meat loaf.

1½	pounds ground veal	⅓	cup pickle relish
1	cup cheddar cheese cut in ¼ inch cubes	¼	cup chopped onion
		1	egg, beaten
¾	cup bread crumbs	1	teaspoon salt
⅓	cup canned evaporated milk	½	teaspoon oregano
		¼	teaspoon pepper

Mix meat with other ingredients and shape into a loaf. Place loaf on a double thickness of heavy-duty foil, just large enough for loaf. Place foil with loaf on smoker grid and water-smoke.

Charcoal: Use 5 pounds charcoal, 3 quarts hot water, 1 wood stick and smoke 1 − 2 hours.
Electric: Use 3 quarts hot water, 1 wood stick and smoke 1 − 2 hours.

Crab Stuffed Veal Steaks

Yield: 4 - 6 servings

This is an excellent stuffing for chicken breasts as well as veal steaks.

2	large veal round steaks, ½-¾ inch thick	2	teaspoons Worcestershire sauce
Salt		1	teaspoon prepared mustard
1	egg, beaten		
1	cup packaged herb seasoned stuffing	¼	teaspoon salt
½	cup cream of mushroom soup	½	cup cream of mushroom soup
1	can (6 ounces) crab meat, drained and flaked	¼	cup oil
		1	teaspoon Kitchen Bouquet
¼	cup chopped green pepper	½	teaspoon onion juice
1	tablespoon lemon juice	Dash pepper	

Season steaks lightly with salt. Lay one steak flat and place other steak on top with only ½ overlapping. Combine in a mixing bowl, next 9 ingredients, mixing well. Place crab mixture in center of steaks and roll up as jelly roll. In another bowl mix last 5 ingredients. Spread veal roll-up with cream of mushroom mixture saving part of mixture to spread on roll-up last 30 minutes of smoking. After roll-up is smoked, heat remainder of cream mixture and serve as gravy for sliced roll-up.

Charcoal: Use 5 pounds charcoal, 3 quarts hot water, 1 wood stick and smoke 2 – 2½ hours.
Electric: Use 3 quarts hot water, 1 wood stick and smoke 1½ – 2 hours.

Lamb can be worked into your menu easily no matter which cut you choose. Today's lamb is young, tender and more meaty than ever before. Overcooking lamb ruins the texture as well as the flavor. Internal temperatures recommended are 140°F rare, 160°F medium and 170°F well done.

Wild Game

Cornish hens, wild duck, pheasant, quail, dove, rabbit, and venison are just a few wild game favorites. You will find several recipes for these such as: Plum Sauce Cornish Hens, Polish Quail, Dakota Wild Duck, Rabbit In Beer and Smoked Venison. The smoker is a hunter's delight!

Stuffed Cornish Hens

Yield: 4 - 6 servings

A prepared rice mix helps make this recipe quick to make.

4 Cornish hens	1 package (7 ounces)
Seasoned salt	Rice-a-Roni
Pepper	

Season hens with seasoned salt and pepper. Prepare rice mix according to package instructions, let cool slightly and stuff hens with mix. Secure openings and place hens on smoker grid.

Charcoal: Use 7 pounds charcoal, 3 quarts hot water, 3 wood sticks and smoke 2 — 3 hours.
Electric: Use 3 quarts hot water, 3 wood sticks and smoke 2 — 3 hours.

Cornish hens are especially good with a sweet fruit sauce. Smoke enhances the flavor. Try using orange wood sticks or other fruit woods for smoking game birds.

Cherry Cornish Hens

Yield: 2 servings

Cornish hens are extra special when smoked. Bing cherries add an elegant look and a pleasing taste.

2 Cornish hens	1½ teaspoon cornstarch
1 can (1 pound) bing	¼ cup orange marmalade
cherries (reserve	¼ cup apricot preserves
½ cup of juice)	

Wash hens and pat dry. Combine ½ cup cherry juice, cornstarch, marmalade and preserves in a saucepan. Heat mixture slowly until thickened and cool slightly. Brush mixture liberally on hens. Place hens on smoker grid and brush once during smoking. Just before serving heat sauce and add drained cherries. Pour cherry sauce over hens to serve.

Charcoal: Use 5 pounds charcoal, 3 quarts hot water, 2 wood sticks and smoke 2 — 2½ hours.
Electric: Use 3 quarts hot water, 2 wood sticks and smoke 2 — 2½ hours.

Cornish Hens With Wild Rice

Yield: 2 servings

Wild rice makes an excellent stuffing for these small hens. The marmalade glaze adds a sweet taste to the meat.

2 Cornish hens	1 cup cooked wild rice
Salt	¼ cup chopped pecans or
¼ cup chopped green	walnuts
onions	½ cup lime marmalade
3 tablespoons butter or	¼ cup orange juice
margarine	

Rinse hens, pat dry and season cavity with salt. Sauté onions in 1 tablespoon butter, stir in rice and chopped nuts. Stuff hens with rice mixture and secure opening. Prepare glaze by melting 2 tablespoons butter in a saucepan. Add marmalade and orange juice, blend until smooth. Brush hens with glaze and place on smoker grid. Brush with glaze before serving.

Charcoal: Use 5 pounds charcoal, 3 quarts hot water, 2 wood sticks and smoke 2 – 2½ hours.
Electric: Use 3 quarts hot water, 2 wood sticks and smoke 2 – 2½ hours.

Fruity Cornish Hens

Yield: 4 - 6 servings

Sugared, seedless grapes are used to stuff these hens. A fruity glaze compliments the flavor of the hens.

4 Cornish hens	¼ cup butter or
Salt	margarine
2 cups seedless green	½ cup apricot preserves
grapes	¼ cup apricot nectar

Rinse hens, pat dry and season with salt. Toss grapes with sugar and stuff each hen with grapes. Melt butter in a saucepan and stir in apricot preserves and nectar. Brush hens with apricot mixture and place on smoker grid. Serve remaining sauce with hens.

Charcoal: Use 7 pounds charcoal, 3 quarts hot water, 3 wood sticks and smoke 2 – 3 hours.
Electric: Use 3 quarts hot water, 3 wood sticks and smoke 2 – 3 hours.

Plum Sauce Cornish Hens

Yield: 4 - 6 servings

This plum sauce gives these small hens a delightful flavor and lovely glaze. The sauce would be good on any small game birds.

4	Cornish game hens	¼	cup melted margarine
	Salt	2	tablespoons orange juice
½	cup Chinese plum sauce, or sweet and sour sauce		

Season cavities of hens with salt. Combine plum sauce, margarine and orange juice. Brush hens with sauce and place on smoker grids to smoke. Brush again after cooking and serve with sauce. Hens on top grid will brown and cook a little faster.

Charcoal: Use 7 pounds charcoal, 3 quarts hot water, 3 wood sticks and smoke 2 — 3 hours.

Electric: Use 3 quarts hot water, 3 wood sticks and smoke 2 — 3 hours.

Tarragon Quail With Limeade

Yield: 4 servings

These game birds usually weigh from 5 to 6 ounces. Being small, quail are usually served 2 to a person or 1 apiece for an appetizer.

8	whole quail	1	can (6 ounces) frozen limeade, thawed
4	tablespoons butter or margarine	1	tablespoon tarragon
2	cloves garlic, minced		Salt and pepper

Rinse quail and pat dry. Melt butter and add remaining ingredients for marinade. Place quail in a dish or heavy-duty plastic bag and pour marinade over quail. Marinate 3-4 hours. Remove quail from marinade and place on smoker grid. Brush quail with marinade before smoking and after removing from the smoker.

Charcoal: Use 5 pounds charcoal, 3 quarts hot water, 1 wood stick and smoke 1 — 2 hours.

Electric: Use 3 quarts hot water, 1 wood stick and smoke 1 — 2 hours.

**Plum Sauce Cornish Hens, Polish Quail,
Barbecued Quail, Smoked Duck with Orange Sauce**

Barbecued Quail

Yield: 4 - 6 servings

Barbecued quail with a hickory smoke flavor.

8-12 quail		¼	cup orange juice
2½	cups barbecue sauce (chunky-style)	1	teaspoon grated orange peel

Wash quail pieces and pat dry. Place quail in two 8-inch square foil pans. Combine barbecue sauce, orange juice and orange peel and pour over quail. Place one foil pan with quail on bottom grid and the other on the top grid and smoke.

Charcoal: Use 5 pounds charcoal, 3 quarts hot water, 2 wood sticks and smoke 1 — 2 hours.

Electric: Use 3 quarts hot water, 2 wood sticks and smoke 1 — 2 hours.

Polish Quail

Yield: 2 per person

Quail, a simple but tasty game bird, is so often pan-fried, but these bacon-wrapped quail are just as good, easy to prepare and there is little clean-up.

Quail	Seasoned Salt
Vegetable oil	Bacon

Rinse quail, pat dry and rub with oil. Season with seasoned salt and wrap with bacon strips. Place bacon-wrapped quail on smoker grid and water-smoke.

Charcoal: Use 5 pounds charcoal, 3 quarts hot water, 1 wood stick and smoke 1 — 2 hours.

Electric: Use 3 quarts hot water, 1 wood stick and smoke 1 — 2 hours.

A lot of the wild game available today is raised specially for the table. If you hunt your own game be certain to take proper care in preparing the game for cooking. Game needs strong seasoning to balance its richness — currant jelly, orange juice, wine and fruits blend well with it. Game birds are usually preferred cooked to well done but venison can be rare or well done.

Quail And Mushrooms

Yield: 4 servings (2 per person)

Here's a country-style dish made easy with canned cream of mushroom soup. This recipe is equally good with dove.

8 quail, split	1 can (10 ounces) condensed cream of mushroom soup
3 tablespoons butter or margarine	
2 cups sliced fresh mushrooms	¼ teaspoon pepper
½ cup chopped onions	½ cup chicken broth (or water)
1 tablespoon Worcestershire sauce	

Split quail in half, wash and pat dry. Place quail in a foil pan or an oven-proof casserole dish. In a large skillet sauté mushrooms and onions until soft, then stir in Worcestershire sauce. Combine mushroom soup, pepper and chicken broth, blend until smooth and pour over quail. Spoon mushrooms and onions on soup mixture and place pan uncovered on smoker grid.

Charcoal: Use 5 pounds charcoal, 3 quarts hot water, 2 wood sticks and smoke 1 — 2 hours.
Electric: Use 3 quarts hot water, 2 wood sticks and smoke 1 — 2 hours.

Roast Dove Maison

Yield: 4 servings

Bacon adds flavor and moistness to these Dove Maison.

8 dove	½ cup Worcestershire sauce
Garlic salt	
Pepper	¼ cup wine
¼ cup lemon juice	Bacon

Rinse dove well and pat dry. Sprinkle inside and out with garlic salt and pepper. Combine lemon juice, Worcestershire sauce, and wine. Marinate dove in lemon juice marinade for several hours. Remove dove from marinade and wrap each with bacon and secure with toothpicks. Place dove on smoker grid and water-smoke.

Charcoal: Use 5 pounds charcoal, 3 quarts hot water, 1 wood stick and smoke 1 — 2 hours.
Electric: Use 3 quarts hot water, 1 wood stick and smoke 1 — 2 hours.

Dijon Smoked Wild Game Birds

Yield: 3 - 4 servings

If someone in your family hunts wild game birds you are fortunate for game birds are at their best smoked.

6-8 small game birds (dove, quail, squab) Dijon mustard	Salt and pepper Bacon

Prepare birds and split in half. Brush birds with a heavy coat of Dijon mustard, season and wrap with bacon. Secure bacon slices with toothpicks. Arrange birds on several pieces of heavy-duty aluminum foil, place on smoker grid and smoke.

Charcoal: Use 5 pounds charcoal, 3 quarts hot water, 2 wood sticks and smoke 1 — 2 hours.

Electric: Use 3 quarts hot water, 2 wood sticks and smoke 1 — 2 hours.

Duck D'Orange

Yield: 6 - 8 servings

Serve Duck D'Orange with wild or brown rice and garnish with mandarin oranges.

4 small ducks 1 can beef consommé, full strength ½ soup can dry sherry ½ can (6 ounces) frozen orange juice concentrate, thawed	½ small jar currant or red plum jelly 2 tablespoons cornstarch dissolved in ½ cup water Brown or wild rice Mandarin oranges

Wash ducks; if large, cut in half to fit in large baking dish or foil pan. Pour consommé and sherry over ducks. Place dish or pan with ducks on smoker grid and smoke. When cooked, remove ducks from smoker and take meat off bones, discarding bones and skin. Stir orange juice and jelly into pan juices. Thicken with cornstarch and water. Return meat to gravy and re-heat in smoker for 20 to 30 minutes. Serve with rice garnished with mandarin oranges.

Charcoal: Use 10 pounds charcoal, 4 — 5 quarts hot water, 3 wood sticks and smoke 4½ — 5½ hours.

Electric: Use 4 quarts hot water, 3 wood sticks and smoke 4 — 5 hours.

Note: Add water to water pan when needed.

Ducks Delight

Yield: 4 servings

A recipe for moist, seasoned duck breast. Everyone will be impressed.

4	ducks, breasted and skinned	1	large green pepper, finely chopped
¼	pound raw bacon coarsely chopped	1	small clove garlic, minced
2	large onions, finely chopped		Salt and pepper

Wash ducks and pat dry. Mix together bacon, onions, green pepper, garlic, salt and pepper. Place duck breasts 2 at a time on a large piece of aluminum foil. Pile equal portions of mixture on top of breast. Wrap foil loosely (do not seal) around duck breast and mixture. Place on smoker grid and water-smoke.

Charcoal: Use 8 – 10 pounds charcoal, 4 quarts hot water, 2 wood sticks and smoke 3½ – 4½ hours.
Electric: Use 4 quarts hot water, 2 wood sticks and smoke 3 – 4 hours.
Note: Add hot water to water pan when needed.

Smoked Duck With Orange Sauce

Yield: 3 - 4 servings

Frozen orange juice concentrate simplifies this classic recipe.

1	5-pound duckling	¼	cup sherry
1	cup frozen orange juice concentrate, thawed	1	clove garlic, minced
½	cup soy sauce	1	teaspoon dry mustard
		¼	teaspoon red hot sauce

Prepare duckling and place in a glass bowl or heavy-duty plastic bag. Combine all the remaining ingredients in a small bowl and pour over duckling, being sure the marinade goes all over the inside as well as the outside of the bird. Cover bowl with plastic wrap or close the bag securely. Refrigerate overnight or for several hours, turning the duckling several times. Remove duckling from refrigerator and place on smoker grid. Prick the surface of the duckling in many places so the fat can drain off. Pour marinade over duckling, cover and smoke. After about 2 hours, baste the duckling. Cook until duck leg twists easily in its socket.

Charcoal: Use 8 pounds charcoal, 4 quarts hot water, 2 wood sticks and smoke 3½ – 4 hours.
Electric: Use 4 quarts hot water, 2 wood sticks and smoke 3 – 3½ hours.
Note: Check water pan and add hot water if needed.

Duckling With Plum Sauce

Yield: 8 servings

Strained plums and lemonade adds a sweet tangy flavor to the ducklings.

2	ducklings (5-6 pounds)	1	can (6 ounces) frozen
	Garlic salt		lemonade
	Onion salt	⅓	cup chili sauce
	4 to 5 large oranges,	¼	cup soy sauce
	sliced	1	teaspoon Worcestershire
⅓	cup butter		sauce
3	jars (4½ ounces)	1	teaspoon ginger
	baby food plums	2	teaspoon prepared
	with tapioca		mustard

Rinse ducks and pat dry. Sprinkle ducks with onion and garlic salt. Place orange slices in an aluminum foil roasting pan or a pan made out of several layers of aluminum foil. Place duck on orange slices. Combine remaining ingredients in a saucepan and simmer for 3-5 minutes. Pour half of mixture over ducks and place pan with ducks on smoker grid. After smoking 3 hours remove ducks, pierce in several places and let excess fat run off. Pour any excess fat out of pan and replace ducks. Pour remaining sauce on ducks and complete cooking.

Charcoal: Use 10 pounds charcoal, 4 quarts hot water, 3 wood sticks and smoke 4 — 5 hours.
Electric: Use 4 quarts hot water, 3 wood sticks and smoke 3½ — 4½ hours.
Note: Add hot water to water pan when needed.

Wild Duck With Orange Sauce

Yield: 2 servings

This is great served with wild or brown rice.

1	medium or large wild duck	1	tablespoon butter
	Salt	¼	cup honey
1	apple, cored and quartered	1	teaspoon orange peel
		¼	teaspoon ginger
		¼	teaspoon basil leaves

To minimize the wild flavor of the duck, you may wish to soak the bird in salted water overnight. Wash the duck and dry with a paper towel. Salt the body, cavity and stuff the duck with apple quarters. In a small saucepan, heat the remaining ingredients until the butter melts. Place the duck in a shallow pan or on a piece of heavy-duty foil large enough to fold completely around the duck. Pour ⅓ of the heated sauce into the cavity and ⅓ over the outside of the duck. Seal all the edges of the foil so the liquid does not drain out but leave an opening. Place bird on smoker grid and water-smoke. After cooking, discard apple and slice meat. Serve with remaining sauce.

Charcoal: Use 7 — 8 pounds charcoal, 3 quarts hot water, 2 wood sticks and smoke 3 — 3½ hours.
Electric: Use 3 quarts hot water, 2 wood sticks and smoke 2½ — 3 hours.

Dakota Wild Duck

Yield: 2 - 3 servings

Wild ducks can be marinated overnight in brandy or red wine to eliminate strong taste.

1	medium or large wild duck		Red and black pepper
8	slivers of garlic	1	large turnip
	Salt	3	slices bacon

Prepare duck and punch holes in each side of the breast (down to the breastbone) and insert one sliver of garlic into each hole. Liberally apply salt, red and black pepper. Insert turnip into cavity of duck. Wrap each strip of bacon completely around duck, secure with toothpicks. Place duck on smoker grid and water-smoke. (Variations: Add wine and bay leaves to water pan.)

Charcoal: Use 7 — 8 pounds charcoal, 4 quarts hot water, 2 wood sticks and smoke 3 — 3½ hours.
Electric: Use 3 quarts hot water, 2 wood sticks and smoke 2½ — 3 hours.

Smoked Pheasant

Yield: 3 - 4 servings

These are good as an entrée and are especially good served cold and sliced with horseradish sauce.

2-3	small pheasants, fully dressed	4	small onions, quartered
1	quart water		Several small sprigs parsley
¼	cup salt	4	tablespoons butter or margarine
12	juniper berries		

Place birds in salt and water, completely submerged for 2 hours in refrigerator. Drain birds, rinse with cold water and let them stand, uncovered, at room temperature for 30 minutes. Put juniper berries, onion and parsley in the cavity of the birds. Brush generously with butter. Place birds on smoker grid and water-smoke.

Charcoal: Use 8 pounds charcoal, 4 quarts hot water, 3 wood sticks and smoke 3½ — 4½ hours.
Electric: Use 4 quarts hot water, 3 wood sticks and smoke 3 — 4 hours.

Fruit-Roasted Pheasant

Yield: 4 servings

This sauce keeps the pheasant moist while imparting a pleasing fruit flavor.

1	large pheasant	½	cup brown rice
	Salt and pepper	1	cup apricot juice
½	cup white rice		

Prepare pheasant and rub interior with salt and pepper. Place pheasant in an aluminum foil pan; cover with the uncooked rice. Pour the fruit juice over rice and pheasant. Smoke-cook until pheasant can be easily pierced with a fork.

Charcoal: Use 7 — 8 pounds charcoal, 4 quarts hot water, 2 wood sticks and smoke 3 — 4 hours.
Electric: Use 4 quarts hot water, 2 wood sticks and smoke 2½ — 3½ hours.

Sweet Smoked Goose

Yield: 6 - 8 servings

Using fruit juices, wine and spices enhances the flavor of smoked birds. This would be a dish for a holiday meal.

1	7-pound goose	*Water Pan*	
Seasoned Salt		1	quart apple cider
1	tablespoon butter	1	cup red wine
⅓	cup honey	3	cinnamon sticks
1	tablespoon apple cider	1	tablespoon whole cloves

Rinse goose, pat dry and season cavity with seasoned salt. Melt butter and stir in honey and cider. Brush mixture over entire bird and place on smoker grid. Prepare smoker by using 3 quarts hot water, apple cider, red wine, cinnamon sticks and cloves in water pan. If available, use fruit wood for smoking.

Charcoal: Use 10 pounds charcoal, 3 quarts hot water, 3 wood sticks and smoke 3½ — 4½ hours.
Electric: Use 2¾ quarts hot water, 3 wood sticks and smoke 3 — 4 hours.
Note: Use ingredients listed above and hot water in water pan.

Teche Country Goose

Yield: 6 - 8 servings

Do not eat the skin of Teche Country Goose, the seasonings make it firey hot!

1	7-pound goose	1	tablespoon salt
1	tablespoon red pepper	1	tablespoon oil
1	tablespoon black pepper	Cola	

Rinse the goose and pat dry. Mix peppers, salt and oil. Add enough cola to make a thick paste. Cover goose with the thick paste and place on smoker grid. Pour remaining cola in water pan.

Charcoal: Use 10 pounds charcoal, 4 quarts hot water, 3 wood sticks and smoke 3½ — 4½ hours.
Electric: Use 4 quarts hot water, 3 wood sticks and smoke 3 — 4 hours.

Rabbit In Beer

Yield: 3 - 4 servings

Marinating the rabbit neutralizes the flavor as well as tenderizes the meat.

1	rabbit, cut up	¼	teaspoon paprika
1	can beer		Salt and pepper
¼	cup chopped onion	3	tablespoons butter,
¼	teaspoon nutmeg		melted

Rinse the rabbit and place in a glass dish or heavy-duty plastic bag. Combine remaining ingredients except butter and pour over rabbit. Marinate for 3-4 hours in refrigerator, turning every hour. Remove rabbit pieces from marinade and place on smoker grid. Brush pieces liberally with melted butter.

Charcoal: Use 5 pounds charcoal, 3 quarts hot water, 1 — 2 wood sticks and smoke 1 — 2 hours.
Electric: Use 3 quarts hot water, 1 — 2 wood sticks and smoke 1 — 2 hours.

Barbecued Rabbit

Yield: 3 - 4 servings

Rabbit has very little fat so it is especially good with a sauce.

1	rabbit, cut-up	¼	cup wine
½	cup currant jelly	½	cup catsup
½	cup chili sauce	1	tablespoon Worcesershire
2	teaspoons Dijon		sauce
	mustard	½	teaspoon salt

Wash rabbit pieces, pat dry and arrange in a shallow dish. Combine remaining ingredients and pour over rabbit pieces. Let set in sauce in refrigerator 1-2 hours. Remove rabbit pieces from sauce and place on smoker grid. Brush liberally with sauce before smoking and just before removing from smoker.

Charcoal: Use 5 pounds charcoal, 3 quarts hot water, 2 wood sticks and smoke 1 — 2 hours.
Electric: Use 3 quarts hot water, 2 wood sticks and smoke 1 — 2 hours.

Marinated Rabbit

Yield: 3 - 4 servings

If a rabbit is part of your catch, try this wine marinated rabbit recipe.

1	rabbit, cut up	1	tablespoon lemon juice
1	cup red wine	½	teaspoon onion powder
2	tablespoons	1	teaspoon thyme
	Worcestershire sauce		Salt and pepper

Rinse rabbit pieces and pat dry. Place rabbit in glass dish or heavy-duty plastic bag. Combine remaining ingredients and pour over rabbit. Marinate 2-3 hours in refrigerator. Remove rabbit from marinade and place on smoker grid to water-smoke.

Charcoal: Use 5 pounds charcoal, 3 quarts hot water, 2 wood sticks and smoke 1 — 2 hours.
Electric: Use 3 quarts hot water, 2 wood sticks and smoke 1 — 2 hours.

Marinated Venison Roast

Yield: 5-6 servings

Marinating helps reduce the gamey flavor of venison.

1	5- to 6-pound venison roast	2	cups dry red wine
	Salt pork, thinly sliced	2	bay leaves
1	clove garlic, crushed	1	bottle Italian salad dressing
	Salt	5	slices bacon
	Freshly ground pepper		

Make slits about 1-inch deep at regular intervals in the roast. Force slices of salt pork into each slit. Rub the roast with garlic, salt and pepper. Place in a large dish and pour wine over meat. Add bay leaves and Italian dressing to the dish and let roast marinate in refrigerator overnight, turning occasionally. Place roast in a roasting pan or foil pan and pour marinade over roast. Place bacon slices over top of roast and place pan with roast on smoker grid. Baste roast thoroughly with marinade at least twice during smoking.

Charcoal: Use 8 — 9 pounds charcoal, 4 — 5 quarts hot water, 3 wood sticks and smoke 4 — 5 hours.
Electric: Use 4 quarts hot water, 3 wood sticks and smoke 3½ — 4½ hours.
Note: Add hot water to water pan when needed.

Smoked Venison Roast

Yield: ¾ pound per serving

For a larger roast increase charcoal, water and cooking time.

1	5- to 6-pound venison roast	1	tablespoon peppercorns
2	cloves garlic, thinly sliced	3	red peppers, chopped
1	cup wine vinegar	1	teaspoon whole cloves
3	cups water	2	ribs celery, chopped
			Bacon strips
		1	onion, chopped

With a sharp knife make slits in the roast and place garlic slices in the slits. Salt roast and place in an enamel or glass pan. Mix remaining ingredients and pour over roast. Marinate roast 8-12 hours, turning frequently. Remove roast from marinade. Place bacon strips over meat and place meat on smoker grid. Baste meat with marinade before and once or twice during smoking.

Charcoal: Use 8 — 9 pounds charcoal, 4 — 5 quarts hot water, 3 wood sticks and smoke 4 — 5 hours.
Electric: Use 4 quarts hot water, 3 wood sticks and smoke 3½ — 4½ hours.
Note: Add hot water to water pan when needed.

Barbecued Venison

Yield: 4 - 6 servings

This marinade also makes a very good sauce.

1	4- to 5-pound venison roast	1	cup red wine
2	cups barbecue sauce	1	bottle (8 ounces) Italian salad dressing

Rinse roast well and place in an enamel or glass dish. Mix remaining ingredients and pour over roast. Cover dish and marinate overnight. Remove roast from marinade and place on smoker grid. Brush with marinade before, once during and after smoking. Serve remaining marinade as a sauce with roast.

Charcoal: Use 8 pounds charcoal, 4 quarts hot water, 2 wood sticks and smoke 3½ — 4½ hours.
Electric: Use 4 quarts hot water, 2 wood sticks and smoke 3 — 4 hours.

Fish & Seafood

Fish from the lakes, rivers, the high seas or local supermarket are at their best when cooked by the moist heat of water-smoking. Beginning with Smoked Salmon, Whole Baked Fish, Pan Fish, or Smoked Crab Legs, Barbecued Frog Legs and Smoked Bouillabaisse all are recipes we recommend.

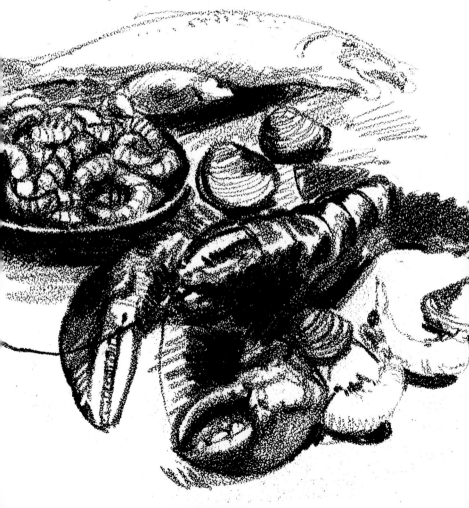

Smoked Salmon

Yield: ⅓ lb. per person

This very expensive delicacy can be made easily and economically at home. Serve hot or cold with Sour Cream Dill Sauce or Sour Cream Cucumber Sauce in Sauces section.

Fresh salmon steaks (about 1 inch thick) or 1 whole salmon Melted butter	Lemon juice Seasoned salt Dill

Salmon Steaks: Combine equal parts of butter and lemon juice and brush each steak on both sides with the mixture. Sprinkle with seasoned salt and dill. Serve with Cucumber Mayonnaise (see note below).

Whole Salmon: Brush salmon cavity with dill and seasoned salt. Repeat on the outside of the salmon. Chill leftover salmon and serve with sour cream and dill or Yogurt-Dill Sauce (see note below).

Salmon Steaks
Charcoal: Use 5 pounds charcoal, 3 quarts hot water, 1 − 2 wood sticks and smoke 1 hour.
Electric: Use 2 quarts hot water, 1 − 2 wood sticks and smoke 1 hour.

Whole Salmon:
Charcoal: Use 7 − 9 pounds charcoal, 4 quarts hot water, 2 wood sticks and smoke 3 − 5 hours (depending on size).
Electric: Use 4 quarts hot water, 2 wood sticks and smoke 3 − 5 hours (depending on size).
Note: Recipes for Cucumber Mayonnaise and Yogurt − Dill Sauce in Sauces section.

Frozen seafood should always be thawed before cooking. The most harm you can do to seafood is to overcook. Seafood is done when the flesh turns white or opaque. The meat will flake easily when forked and shellfish will feel firm to the touch. If cooked in the shell the shells will open when done. Seafood is most delicate and requires short cooking times. Fish with high fat content will require longer cooking.

Smoked Stuffed Salmon

Yield: 4 servings

This is a nice recipe for small whole salmon. Fix this feast for your special guest. Show them what you can do with a smoker!

1	4- to 5-pound drawn, scaled salmon	½	cup dry bread cubes
Oil		¼	cup chopped celery
1	cup chopped peeled tomato	¼	teaspoon salt
¼	cup chopped green onion	½	teaspoon lemon pepper
¼	cup chopped fresh dill	1	small clove garlic, minced

Prepare salmon and brush with oil. Combine remaining ingredients and stuff salmon with this mixture. Place salmon on a sheet of heavy-duty foil that has been doubled and greased. Place on water smoker grid and smoke.

Charcoal: Use 7 pounds charcoal, 4 quarts hot water, 2 wood sticks and smoke 3½ – 4½ hours.
Electric: Use 4 quarts hot water, 2 wood sticks and smoke 3 – 4 hours.

Halibut in Foil

Yield: 4 servings

If your meal is casual, you may wish to serve this fish in the foil packets.

2-3	pounds halibut steaks, fresh or frozen, cut in 4 serving pieces	½	cup chopped onion
Lemon juice		½	cup chopped green pepper
½	teaspoon garlic salt	2	tablespoons butter, cut in pieces
Salt and pepper		¼	cup catsup

Thaw if using frozen fish. Cut 4 pieces of foil approximately 10 inches long and fold in half. Turn edges up on each piece and fold corners so juices cannot drip. Place 1 serving of fish in center of each foil piece and sprinkle with lemon juice, garlic salt, salt and pepper. Top each with onion, green pepper, butter and catsup. Place fish in foil on smoker grid and water-smoke.

Charcoal: 3 – 5 pounds charcoal, 3 quarts hot water, 1 wood stick and smoke 1 – 1½ hours.
Electric: Use 2 quarts hot water, 1 wood stick and smoke 1 – 1½ hours.

Baked Garlic Trout

Yield: 4 servings

A nice way to prepare fresh trout with herbs.

2 whole, cleaned trout (or any other white fish)	1 tablespoon minced parsley
	1 teaspoon minced onion
Salt and pepper	¼ cup white wine
¼ cup butter, softened	1 tablespoon lemon juice
¼ clove garlic, crushed	Chopped parsley for garnish

Sprinkle the trout with salt and pepper. Set aside. Cream together the next four ingredients. Spoon half of mixture into cavity of each trout. Place fish in a shallow baking dish or foil pan. Combine wine and lemon juice and pour over the trout. Place pan with fish on smoker grid and water-smoke. Spoon remaining juices in pan over the fish and serve garnished with chopped parsley.

Charcoal: Use 5 pounds charcoal, 3 quarts hot water, ,1 wood stick and smoke 1½ – 2 hours.

Electric: Use 3 quarts hot water, 1 wood stick and smoke 1½ – 2 hours.

Baked Lemon Trout

Yield: 4 - 6 servings

This is for fishermen at the scene.

4 trout, prepared as described below	½ cup chopped fresh parsley
	2 ounces dry vermouth
¼ cup butter, melted	Salt
Juice of 2 lemons	

Leave heads of fish intact. Slit fish with a sharp knife from the gills down. Remove entrails and wash well.

Mix butter, lemon juice, parsley and vermouth. Pour this marinade into a shallow glass baking dish. Add fish. Marinate for 1½ hours, turning once. Remove fish from marinade and salt well. Place fish cut side down (they will resemble small tents) in baking pan or in foil pan. Pour marinade over top and place pan on smoker grid.

Charcoal: Use 5 pounds charcoal, 3 quarts hot water, 1 wood stick and smoke 1½ – 2½ hours.

Electric: Use 3 quarts hot water , 1 wood stick and smoke 1½ – 2 hours.

Baked Lemon Trout, New Orleans
Peppered Shrimp, Smoked Whole Lobster

Fish in Herbs

Yield: 3 - 5 servings

The delicate flavor of fish improves with the subtle addition of smoke. You can stuff a large fish using your favorite stuffing recipe.

1	3- to 4-pound flounder, haddock, sea bass or mackerel	¼	teaspoon each thyme, tarragon, rosemary
2	onions, chopped	6	tablespoons butter or margarine, melted
2	stalks celery, chopped		Parmesan cheese
1	cup sliced mushrooms		
2	tablespoons chopped parsley		

Thaw if using frozen fish. Mix together the onions, celery, mushrooms, parsley and herbs with melted butter. Spread half of mixture in a greased baking dish or on several layers of heavy-duty foil to form a container. Place fish on top of vegetable mixture and sprinkle with Parmesan cheese. Top with remaining mixture and place on smoker grid. Baste with butter after smoking.

Charcoal: Use 5 pounds charcoal, 3 quarts hot water, 1 wood stick and smoke 1½ — 2 hours.

Electric: Use 3 quarts hot water, 1 wood stick and smoke 1½ — 2 hours.

Pan Fish

Yield: 4 - 6 servings

After tasting smoke-cooked fish you will understand why fishermen like to take their smokers along on fishing trips.

6	small whole pan fish, fresh or frozen (perch, sunfish, bluegills, crappie)		Freshly ground pepper or lemon pepper
		¼	cup oil

If frozen, thaw fish. Sprinkle cavities of the fish with pepper or lemon pepper. Brush outsides of fish with oil. Place fish on smoker grid and water-smoke.

Charcoal: Use 3 — 5 pounds charcoal, 2 quarts hot water, 1 — 2 wood sticks and smoke 45 minutes to 1 hour.

Electric: Use 2 quarts hot water, 1 — 2 wood sticks and smoke 45 minutes to 1 hour.

Fillets Au Gratin

Yield: 6 servings

These fillets are smoked with a tasty coating of cheese. Serve with tartar sauce, seafood cocktail sauce or barbecue sauce.

3 pounds perch, flounder, cod or other firm fish fillets, fresh or frozen	1 tablespoon lemon juice
	1 clove garlic, minced
¼ cup oil	1 cup shredded cheddar cheese
1 teaspoon salt	1 cup fine bread, cracker or cereal crumbs
½ teaspoon white pepper	

Thaw if using frozen fish. Cut fish into serving portions. Combine oil, salt, pepper, lemon and garlic. Mix shredded cheese and crumbs. Dip each piece of fish in oil mixture and roll in cheese-crumb mixture. Place fish on heavy-duty foil that has been doubled and greased. Place foil with fish on smoker grid and water-smoke. Serve with tartar sauce, seafood cocktail sauce or barbecue sauce.

Charcoal: Use 5 pounds charcoal, 3 quarts hot water, 1 wood stick and smoke 1 – 1½ hours.

Electric: Use 2 quarts hot water, 1 wood stick and smoke 1 – 1½ hours.

Smoke Baked Bass

Yield: 6 servings

This pan smoked fish has a nice seasoned cream sauce. A nice recipe to try with your week-end catch.

12 pieces of fillet of bass or other white fish	¼ cup chopped green onion and tops
1 can (10 ounces) cream of celery soup	¼ cup butter or margarine
½ cup water	½ cup grated yellow cheese
¼ cup chopped parsley	

Prepare fish and set aside. Mix soup and water together and pour into a baking dish, foil pan or heavy-duty foil fashioned into a baking dish. Arrange fish in dish or foil pan and sprinkle with parsley and onion. Dot with the butter and sprinkle cheese on top. Place on smoker grid, uncovered if you want a smoke flavor.

Charcoal: Use 5 pounds charcoal, 3 quarts hot water, 1 wood stick and smoke 1½ – 2 hours.

Electric: Use 3 quarts hot water, 1 wood stick and smoke 1½ – 2 hours.

Whole Baked Fish — Creole Style

Yield: 6 servings

For large whole fish plan on about 3 servings from 2 pounds of fish.

1 4- to 5-pound whole fish, scaled, drawn, split and cleaned (red snapper, lemon fish, striped bass, flounder, mackerel, etc.)	¼ cup chopped parsley
	1 can (1 pound) tomatoes, chopped
Juice of one lemon	2 bay leaves
Sauce	½ teaspoon thyme
¼ cup butter or margarine	½ teaspoon basil
¼ cup oil	¼ teaspoon cayenne pepper
½ cup flour	1 teaspoon salt
1 onion, chopped	1 teaspoon seasoned pepper
2 cloves garlic, minced	2 tablespoons lemon juice
	½ cup water

Sprinkle fish with lemon juice inside and out several hours before cooking and refrigerate. In a heavy saucepan melt butter and add oil. Gradually add flour and cook over low heat, stirring constantly. Cook until a golden brown roux begins to form. Add onion, garlic and parsley, continue to cook while stirring constantly. Remove from heat, add tomatoes, herbs, salt, pepper and water, stirring well. Return to heat and cook on low heat for 15 minutes. Remove bay leaves. Pour ⅓ of sauce in a large foil roasting pan, put in fish which has been scored diagonally in 4 inch cuts across grain. Pour another ⅓ sauce over fish and place foil pan on smoker grid. Serve fish with remaining ¹/ sauce and decorate with lemon slices, sliced ripe olives and parsley.

Charcoal: Use 5 — 7 pounds charcoal, 3 quarts hot water, 2 wood sticks and smoke 2 — 3 hours.

Electric: Use 3 quarts hot water, 2 wood sticks and smoke 2 — 2½ hours.

Smoked Sweet and Sour Shrimp

Yield: 4 - 6 servings

Superbly delicious!

2	pounds fresh shrimp, in shells	1	tablespoon chopped pimento
1	cup sugar	½	teaspoon salt
½	cup white vinegar	2	teaspoons cornstarch
½	cup water	1	tablespoon cool water
1	tablespoon chopped green pepper	1	teaspoon paprika

Wash and drain shrimp. Combine next 6 ingredients in a saucepan and simmer at low for 5 minutes. Combine cornstarch and cool water then pour into hot mixture and stir until sauce thickens. Remove from heat and cool. When cool, add paprika. Place shrimp in a shallow glass dish or heavy-duty plastic bag. Pour sauce over shrimp and marinate 2-3 hours. Remove shrimp from sauce and place on smoker grid and brush again with sauce. For serving, place shrimp in dish and pour heated sauce over shrimp. These can be placed on foil or skewers for easier handling.

Charcoal: Use 3 pounds charcoal, 2 quarts hot water, 1 wood stick and smoke 30 to 45 minutes.
Electric: Use 2 quarts hot water, 1 wood stick and smoke 30 to 45 minutes.

New Orleans Peppered Shrimp

Yield: 6 - 8 servings

Remember, shrimp are ready to eat when they turn bright pink.

2-3	pounds large or jumbo shrimp in shells	1	bottle (8 ounces) Italian dressing
1½	sticks butter or margarine	1½	tablespoons ground pepper
	Juice of 1 large lemon		

Wash shrimp in colander. Melt butter and pour in large baking dish or foil pan. Stir in lemon juice, dressing and pepper. Then add shrimp, tossing to coat. Place pan on smoker grid. Stir shrimp once during smoking and after removing from smoker.

Charcoal: Use 3 – 5 pounds charcoal, 2 quarts hot water, 2 wood sticks and smoke 45 minutes to 1 hour.
Electric: Use 2 quarts hot water, 2 wood sticks and smoke 45 minutes to 1 hour.

Smoked King Crab Legs

Yield: 6 main dish or 12 appetizer servings

Serve this as an éntrée or appetizer. Fit for a KING!

3	pounds frozen Alaskan king crab legs, thawed	2	tablespoons white wine
¼	cup melted butter	1	tablespoon lemon juice

After crab legs have thawed, combine melted butter (it is best to use butter, not margarine), wine and lemon juice. Prepare smoker and place crab legs on top smoker grid. Brush generously with butter mixture. Smoke just until crab meat is white and firm. For dipping sauce, double sauce recipe above.

Charcoal: Use 3—5 pounds charcoal, 2 quarts hot water, 1 wood stick and smoke 45 minutes to 1 hour.
Electric: Use 2 quarts hot water, 1 wood stick and smoke 45 minutes to 1 hour.
Note: The meat of the crab legs is quite delicate so be careful not to overcook. In very warm weather, cooking time may be shortened.

Italian Crab Legs

Yield: 6 servings

The Italian dressing adds a pungent flavor. Be careful not to marinate too long or smoke too long.

3	pounds crab legs	Butter
1	bottle Italian salad dressing	Lemon

If frozen, thaw crab legs. Place crab legs in a large shallow dish or plastic bag. Pour Italian dressing over crab legs and let set in dressing one hour. To absorb more flavor, crack the crab legs in several places. Do not marinate longer than one hour. Remove crab legs from dressing and place on smoker grid to smoke. Serve with lemon wedges and melted butter.

Charcoal: Use 3 pounds charcoal, 2 quarts hot water, 1 wood stick and smoke 45 minutes to 1 hour.
Electric: Use 2 quarts hot water, 1 wood stick and smoke 45 minutes to 1 hour.
Note: Do not overcook. Five pounds charcoal will smoke 3 to 6 pounds crab legs.

Lobster Tails

Yield: 1 per person

If you prefer, the wood sticks can be eliminated for slow-cook steaming. If you want a little smoke flavor add only 1 wood stick.

Lobster tails	1 teaspoon Worcestershire
Butter, melted	sauce
Lemon wedges (optional)	½ tablespoon curry powder
Tomato-Curry Baste	½ teaspoon salt
2 tablespoons butter	¼ teaspoon pepper
2 tablespoons flour	1 small onion, minced
2 cups tomato juice or	1 teaspoon sugar
canned tomatoes	

If frozen, thaw lobster tails. Cut underside membrane. Grasp tail in both hands and crack shell firmly to prevent curling. Brush flesh with melted butter and place shell side down on grid nearest water pan. After a few minutes, turn and brush again with butter. Serve with lemon wedges and butter, or Tomato-Curry Baste.

To make baste, melt butter and blend in flour. Stir in remaining ingredients and simmer 15 minutes. Cool and refrigerate until ready to serve. Use as a baste or dip for lobster or fish. Serve warm.

Charcoal: Use 3 pounds charcoal, 2 quarts hot water, wood stick optional, smoke 30 to 45 minutes.
Electric: Use 2 quarts hot water, wood stick optional and smoke 30 – 45 minutes.

Sweet Sesame Frog Legs

Yield: 6 servings (2 per person)

Unusual, but oh so good! Don't overcook or they will be too dry.

12 frog legs (approximately	⅔ cup honey
2½ pounds)	¼ teaspoon salt
½ cup soy sauce	Sesame seeds, toasted
¼ cup butter or margarine	

Marinate frog legs in soy sauce 4 to 5 hours. Remove frog legs from sauce and pat dry. Reserve ¼ cup soy sauce. Melt butter and combine with honey, salt and soy sauce. Dip frog legs in honey mixture, thoroughly coating each. Roll frog legs in toasted sesame seeds and place directly on the smoker grid or on a sheet of greased heavy-duty foil. Place foil with frog legs on smoker grid and smoke.

Charcoal: Use 5 pounds charcoal, 3 quarts hot water, 1 wood stick and smoke 1 – 2 hours.
Electric: Use 3 quarts hot water, 1 wood stick and smoke 1 – 2 hours.

Barbecued Frog Legs

Yield: 6 servings (2 per person)

Use your favorite barbecue sauce or try this one with a base of bottled seafood cocktail sauce.

12	frog legs	1	tablespoon brown sugar
⅔	cup seafood cocktail sauce	¼	cup finely chopped green pepper
⅓	cup catsup	1	teaspoon prepared mustard
2	tablespoons Worcestershire sauce		

Rinse frog legs and pat dry. Place frog legs in a shallow heat-proof dish or foil pan. Combine remaining ingredients and pour over frog legs. Let frog legs stay in sauce 3-4 hours in refrigerator. Place dish or foil pan on smoker grid and water-smoke.

Charcoal: Use 5 pounds chracoal, 3 quarts hot water, 1 wood stick and smoke 1 — 2 hours.
Electric: Use 3 quarts hot water, 1 wood stick and smoke 1 — 2 hours.

White Fish Mousse

Yield: 8 - 10 appetizers or first course servings

Serve this as a first course or appetizer. This can be served warm or cold and will freeze well.

1½	pounds white fish fillet, skins removed	½	teaspoon white pepper
½	cup egg whites		Dash seasonings
1	cup cream		Watercress or parsley

Line a loaf pan with greased parchment paper. With the metal blade in a food processor, process the white fish fillet (all bone removed) until finely chopped. In a separate bowl, beat the egg whites until quite stiff. Add the cream to the fish in the processor and continue to process until the mixture is very smooth. Add the seasonings. Fold into egg whites and pour into prepared pan. Put the loaf pan on the smoker grid. After smoking, remove pan from smoker and let set about 10 minutes before unmolding.

Charcoal: Use 5 pounds charcoal, 3 quarts hot water, 1 wood stick and smoke 1½ — 2 hours.
Electric: Use 3 quarts hot water, 1 wood stick and smoke 1½ — 2 hours.

Smoked Bouillabaisse

Yield: 6 servings

If you really want to impress your guests, serve this special seafood dish. This bouillabaisse recipe makes an affordable amount, enough for 6.

8	ounces lobster tails	1	cup water
10	ounces red snapper or sole fillets	1	can (16 ounces) tomatoes, cut up
10	ounces cod, perch or haddock fillets	¼	cup snipped parsley
8	ounces scallops	1	bay leaf
8	ounces shrimp, medium	1	teaspoon dried thyme
1	pound clams in shells	3	strips orange rind,
1½	cups chopped onion		2 inches long,
1	clove garlic, minced		⅛ inch wide
2	tablespoons olive oil	2	teaspoons salt
		2-3	drops of red hot sauce

Thaw frozen fish and shellfish. Cut lobster in half lengthwise; cut crosswise to make 6 pieces. (You might want to get your butcher to do this but you can do it yourself with a large sharp knife). Cut blocks of fish fillets into 1 inch pieces. Wash shrimp well but leave in shell. Wash clams well. Place all fish and shellfish in a foil roasting pan and set aside. Sauté onions and garlic in oil until soft. Combine remaining ingredients adding onions and garlic. Pour this mixture over fish and shellfish. Place pan on smoker grid and water-smoke. Serve immediately after smoking; fish will continue to cook in hot juices. Bouillabaisse is usually served with buttered French bread, but rice is good too.

Charcoal: Use 5 pounds charcoal, 3 quarts hot water, 2 wood sticks and smoke 1 hour.
Electric: Use 3 quarts hot water, 2 wood sticks and smoke 1 hour.

Appetizers and Kabobs

Smoked Chicken Drummies, Fahita, Smoked Stuffed Mushrooms, Eggplant Caviar and Smoked Curry Pecans are just a few tempting tidbits we hope you enjoy. Don't forget those favorite kabobs such as Kuwait Lamb Kabobs, Shrimp and Scallop Kabobs or Thrifty Barbecued Shish Kabobs.

Smoked Chicken Drummies

Yield: 4 - 5 per person as an entrée, 3 per person as an appetizer

Drummies are the meaty portion of the wing. With the boney sections removed, these wings resemble small drumsticks.

2 dozen chicken drummies (meaty portion of wing)	Oil Seasoned salt

Ask your butcher to cut the drummies from the chicken wings. Rinse chicken and pat dry. Brush drummies with oil and sprinkle with seasoned salt. Place directly on smoker grid or on skewer for ease in handling and water-smoke.

Charcoal: Use 3 pounds charcoal, 2 quarts hot water, 1 — 2 wood sticks and smoke 30 to 45 minutes.
Electric: Use 2 quarts hot water, 1 — 2 wood sticks and smoke 30 to 45 minutes.

Glazed Chicken Wings

Yield: 4 servings, 6 - 8 servings as an appetizer

Inexpensive, but very tasty. Make full use of your water-smoker and smoke these glazed wings along with a turkey, ham or spareribs.

12   chicken wings
      (approx. 3 pounds)
Seasoned salt
Pepper
½ cup butter or margarine
	1 jar (12 ounces) apricot
	      preserves
	¼ cup English mustard
	¼ cup brown sugar

Rinse chicken wings, pat dry and season with seasoned salt and pepper. Lock wing tips so they will be more compact. Combine remaining ingredients in a saucepan and heat until well blended. Cool 10 minutes. Coat wings thoroughly with glaze and place on smoker grid. Brush with glaze again after 30 minutes of cooking and after cooking is completed.

Charcoal: Use 3 — 5 pounds charcoal, 3 quarts hot water, 1 wood stick and smoke 1 — 1½ hours.
Electric: Use 2 quarts hot water, 1 wood stick, and smoke 1 — 1½ hours.

**Chicken Drummies, Smoked Sausage, Smoked Swiss Cheese,
Smoked Cheddar Cheese, Smoked Party Mix**

Bologna Roast

Yield: 6 servings

An interesting picnic roast. Serve same as baked ham. Slice leftovers for sandwiches.

1	2½- to 3-pound bologna, unsliced	1	cup plum or currant jelly
	Cloves	1	teaspoon lemon juice
	Pineapple slices	⅔	cup brown sugar
	Maraschino cherries	1	teaspoon dry mustard
		1	tablespoon water

Score bologna as you would a ham. Stud with cloves and decorate with pineapple and cherries securing with toothpicks. Combine remaining ingredients in a saucepan and heat until jelly melts. Pour glaze over bologna. Save glaze and brush on roast after cooking. Place bologna on smoker grid and smoke.

Charcoal: Use 5 pounds charcoal, 3 quarts hot water, 2 − 3 wood sticks and smoke 2 − 2½ hours.
Electric: Use 3 quarts hot water, 2 − 3 wood sticks and smoke 2 − 2½ hours.

Beef Jerky

Yield: about 1½ pounds

Beef jerky makes a nice snack or appetizer and is great for picnics, camping and backpacking trips.

2	pounds flank steak	1	clove garlic,
⅓	cup soy sauce		minced (optional)

Trim all visible fat from the steak (jerky keeps indefinitely if all fat is trimmed). Cut the flank steak, lengthwise with the grain, into long thin strips, ¼ inch thick. Place the strips in a bowl, pour soy sauce over the meat, and toss several times. Marinate 15 minutes. Place strips on smoker grids, leaving a small space between each. Refrigerate after smoking.

Charcoal: Use 3 − 5 pounds charcoal, 3 quarts hot water, 2 wood sticks and smoke 1 − 1½ hours.
Electric: Use 2 quarts hot water, 2 wood sticks and smoke 1 − 1½ hours.

Smoked Fresh Sausages

As much as 6 pounds of sausage can be smoked according to instructions below.

Use any uncooked sausages such as:

German   Knockwurst
Polish   Bratwurst
Italian

Cut slits in sausages, if desired, for more smoke flavor. Place sausages on smoker grid and water-smoke.

Charcoal: Use 5 pounds charcoal, 3 quarts hot water, 2 wood sticks and smoke 1 — 2 hours.
Electric: Use 3 quarts hot water, 2 wood sticks and smoke 1 — 2 hours.

Fahita

Yield: 4 - 6 servings

This marinated steak is super when smoked over mesquite wood. It could be used as a main course or appetizer. If your butcher doesn't have the skirt steak, use a flank steak.

1	1½-pound skirt steak	⅓	cup tequila
	Meat tenderizer	3	tablespoons brown sugar
¼	cup teriyaki sauce	¾	cup water

Sprinkle steak with meat tenderizer. Mix remaining ingredients and pour over steak. Marinate overnight or as long as 24 hours. Place steak on smoker grid and smoke using mesquite wood.

Charcoal: Use 3 — 5 pounds charcoal, 3 quarts hot water, 2 wood sticks and smoke 1 — 1½ hours.
Electric: Use 2 quarts hot water, 2 wood sticks and smoke 1 — 1½ hours.

Skirt Steak

Smoked Stuffed Mushrooms

Yield: 6 - 8 appetizer servings

24	large mushrooms with caps (about 1-inch across)	½	teaspoon pepper
¼	pound small mushrooms	¼	teaspoon garlic salt
¾	cup grated cheddar cheese	¼	teaspoon Italian seasoning
1	teaspoon Worcestershire sauce	¼	cup bread crumbs
½	teaspoon salt	¼	cup butter or margarine
2	green onions, finely chopped		Dash of Tabasco
		½	teaspoon Worcestershire
			Paprika

Clean and remove stems from large mushrooms, set caps aside. Clean small mushrooms then chop stems and small mushrooms very fine. Mix together chopped mushrooms, cheese, Worcestershire, salt, pepper, garlic salt, Italian seasonings and bread crumbs. Melt butter and add dash of Tabasco and ½ teaspoon Worcestershire. Brush liberally inside of large mushroom caps with butter mixture. Add remaining butter to chopped mixture and mix all together. Stuff caps with mushroom mixture and sprinkle with paprika. Place caps on a double thickness of heavy-duty foil and place on smoker grid. Smoke for 45 minutes or until well heated.

Marinated Vegetables and Mushrooms

Delicious with smoked meats — serve as an appetizer or salad.

½	pound fresh mushrooms	2	cups cauliflower flowerettes
2-3	raw carrots		
3	cups broccoli flowerettes	1	bottle (16 ounces) Italian salad dressing

Wash mushrooms and vegetables. Remove stems from mushrooms and slice carrots ¼-½ inch thick. Boil mushrooms and carrots until mushrooms are firm and carrots are just beginning to soften. Immerse cauliflower in boiling water for about 3-4 minutes and broccoli for about 1-2 minutes (not too long or broccoli will darken). Drain all vegetables and rinse with ice water. Place vegetables in a shallow container, pour Italian dressing over all and seal. Refrigerate overnight before serving. More vegetables can be added to dressing after serving.

Smoked Stuffed Artichoke

Yield: 4 servings

These are so nice to serve at a special dinner. Cook them in boiling water, stuff and smoke.

4	artichokes	3	tablespoons white wine
2	green onions, finely chopped	3	tablespoons lemon juice
6	tablespoons olive oil		Salt and pepper
1	cup mushrooms, finely chopped	½	teaspoon garlic salt
½	cup bread crumbs	½	cup finely chopped, cooked ham
¼	cup Parmesan cheese	1	tablespoon chopped parsley

Trim tops and leaves of artichokes with scissors and cut stalks level with base. Put artichokes into a kettle of boiling salted water and simmer about 35-40 minutes or until a leaf can be pulled out easily. Drain, refresh under cold running water, and let stand upside down until cool. To make the dressing: sauté green onions slowly in 2 tablespoons of the oil, until just tender. Stir in mushrooms and cook 2-3 minutes; then stir in bread crumbs and cheese. Transfer mixture to a bowl and let stand until cool. Stir in wine, lemon juice and remaining oil. Season well with garlic salt, salt and pepper, then add ham. Prepare each artichoke by pulling out some of the center leaves until the choke can be reached. With a teaspoon, scrape out all the hairy choke. Fill each artichoke with dressing and top with parsley. Wrap each artichoke in foil leaving the top open. Place on smoker grid and smoke for 1-1½ hours.

Smoked Almonds and Pecans

Smoke these in large quantities for gifts.

5½	ounces raw almonds	4	drops of Tabasco sauce
5½	ounces pecans	1	tablespoon Worcestershire sauce
1	teaspoon seasoned salt	1	tablespoon oil
¼	teaspoon garlic powder		
¼	teaspoon onion powder		

Mix the above, tossing well. Put in a foil pan and place on smoker grid. Smoke slowly for about 1½-2 hours, stirring twice. (Make certain you are using at least 2 wood sticks.)

Smoked Curry Pecans

All nuts can be smoked using a little oil or butter and seasonings, if desired. These Curry Pecans are super tasting.

2	cups shelled pecans		Curry powder
2	tablespoon butter or margarine, melted	½	cup Dr. Pepper

Place pecans in a foil pan and toss with melted butter. Sprinkle pecans with curry powder and toss again. Pour in Dr. Pepper and place on smoker grid. Smoke for 1½-2 hours or until liquid is all absorbed. If you are only smoking nuts, don't forget to use at least 2 wood sticks for smoke flavor.

Smoker Party Mix

Those people who love to nibble on snacks will love this cereal mix with Taco Seasoning and a hint of smoke flavor.

½	cup butter or margarine	2	cups bite-size wheat cereal
2	tablespoons Taco Seasoning mix	2	cups bite-size shredded wheat
1	teaspoon salt	1	cup pretzel sticks
3	tablespoons Worcestershire	1	cup salted mixed nuts
2	cups bite-size corn or rice cereal		

Melt butter and add Taco Seasoning, salt and Worcestershire sauce. In a large foil roasting pan mix cereals, pretzel sticks and nuts. Pour butter mixture over cereal mixture and toss well. Place pan, uncovered, on smoker grid. Smoke-cook this snack without the water-pan. Use one <u>small</u> wood stick (when the wood stick burns the smoker might get too hot if the wood is large). It is best not to smoke other foods with this cereal snack since there is no water pan and you must open the smoker every 15 minutes to stir the cereal.

Charcoal: Use 2 — 3 pounds charcoal (do not use more), no water pan, 1 small wood stick and smoke 45 minutes or until liquid is absorbed.

Electric: Use no water pan, 1 small wood stick and smoke 45 minutes or until liquid is absorbed.

Note: Stir cereal mix every 15 minutes.

Smoked Cheese

A very delicious treat, smoked cheese is great for parties and snacks. The secret to smoking cheese is low heat. This must be done with close attention or the cheese will melt. The cheese absorbs the smoke flavor very quickly.

2   slabs (about 8 ounces   Paprika (optional)
     or larger) cheese such   Caraway seeds (optional)
     as Swiss, Cheddar,   Chili powder (optional)
     Edam, Colby or
     Monterey Jack

Prepare a double thickness of heavy-duty foil large enough to hold cheese. Poke holes in foil. If desired, sprinkle cheese with paprika, caraway seeds or chili powder. Place cheese on foil and place on smoker grid. Procedures for smoking vary with smokers, so read instructions carefully.

Charcoal: Use about 6 charcoal briquettes, 7 quarts COOL water, 4 slivers of wood and smoke about 45 minutes to 1 hour.
Electric: Preheat with 2 quarts COOL water and 1 wood stick. When wood starts smoking add 2 quarts COOL water, place cheese on bottom grid of smoker and smoke 20 – 30 minutes.
Note: Check at intervals to make sure the cheese is not melting.

Eggplant Caviar

Serve on party crackers or as a dip. This one will surprise you — always a favorite at parties. It is made easy by cooking the eggplant in the water smoker.

1   medium eggplant   2   tablespoons oil
½   cup finely chopped onion   2   tablespoons vinegar
1   clove garlic, minced   1   teaspoon sugar
1   tomato, peeled, seeded   Salt and pepper
     and chopped fine   4   tablespoons chopped
¼   cup finely chopped   fresh parsley
     bell pepper

Wash eggplant and place on smoker grid. Cook for about 2 hours or until the eggplant gets soft and has collapsed. Chill eggplant, then peel and mash. Add other ingredients except parsley. Place eggplant in a serving bowl and sprinkle parsley on top. Chill and serve with party crackers or chips.

Oysters Rockefeller Casserole

Yield: 4 servings

This is a nice appetizer to smoke with meats.

1	package frozen, chopped spinach, defrosted		Dash garlic salt
½	cup fresh parsley	¾	stick butter, melted
½	cup chives, snipped	1	pint oysters
½	teaspoon Tabasco	½	cup bread crumbs
1	teaspoon Worcestershire sauce	¼	cup Parmesan cheese

Mix first seven ingredients together. Then fold in oysters and put into a foil pan or casserole dish. Combine bread crumbs and Parmesan cheese, sprinkle over oyster mixture. These will cook in 1 to 1½ hours in the smoker.

Beef Kabobs

Yield: 4 servings

For best results select foods for kabobs that cook in about the same time or parboil those that require longer cooking time.

1	pound lean boneless beef (top round or sirloin tip)	1	red pepper
		¼	cup oil
2	onions	¼	cup teriyaki sauce
2	green peppers	¼	cup red wine
			Salt and pepper

Cut beef in 1½-inch cubes. Peel onions and cut in wedges large enough to skewer. Remove seeds from peppers and cut in squares. Combine remaining ingredients and pour over beef and vegetables. Marinate beef and vegetables for 1 hour in refrigerator. Remove from marinade and skewer, alternating each item. Brush again with marinade and place on smoker grid and water-smoke.

Charcoal Use 3–5 pounds charcoal, 2 quarts hot water, 1–2 wood sticks and smoke 45 minutes to 1 hour.

Electric Use 2 quarts hot water, 1–2 wood sticks and smoke 45 minutes to 1 hour.

Kabobs

Kuwait Lamb Kabobs

Yield: 4 servings

Kabobs require less smoking time than roast and are a great idea for short-notice guest.

1½	pounds lean lamb, cut into 1½-inch cubes	¼	teaspoon cloves
¼	cup olive oil	¼	teaspoon cinnamon
½	cup peanut oil	¼	teaspoon allspice
¼	cup lemon juice	3	quartered, medium onions
¼	cup dry red wine	1	unpeeled eggplant, cut into 1-inch cubes
½	cup chopped green onion	1	tablespoon finely chopped mint
1	teaspoon pepper		
1	clove garlic, minced		

Marinate lamb cubes for at least 3 hours in a mixture of the oils, lemon juice, wine, green onion, pepper, garlic, cloves, cinnamon and allspice. Remove lamb from marinade. Spear quartered onion, lamb, and eggplant on four 14-inch skewers, alternating each until skewers are filled. Brush liberally with marinade and place skewers on smoker grid. Sprinkle with mint before serving.

Charcoal: Use 3 — 5 pounds charcoal, 2 quarts hot water, 1 — 2 wood sticks and smoke 1 hour.
Electric: Use 2 quarts hot water, 1 — 2 wood sticks and smoke 1 hour.

Shrimp and Scallop Kabobs

Yield: 4 servings

Serve with brown rice, cole slaw, hot Italian bread and a dry white wine.

1	pound large shrimp	1	teaspoon dry dill
1	pound large scallops		Lemon pepper marinade
6	slices bacon	6	halved large fresh mushrooms
1	stick butter		Parsley to garnish
	Juice of ½ lemon		

Shell and devein shrimp. If desired leave in shells for more tender texture. Leave tails on. Cut bacon slices in half and wrap half strip around each scallop. Melt butter, add lemon juice and dry dill. Season to taste with lemon pepper. Marinate shrimp, scallops and mushrooms in butter mixture approximately 2 hours. On each of 4 skewers spear first a shrimp, next a mushroom, half, then a wrapped scallop. Repeat, ending with a shrimp. Smoke until shrimp turn bright pink and scallops are white. Serve with butter mixture. Garnish with parsley sprigs.

Charcoal: Use 3 pounds charcoal, 2 quarts hot water, 1 wood stick and smoke about 30 – 45 minutes.
Electric: Use 2 quarts hot water, 1 wood stick and smoke 30 – 45 minutes.

Ratatouille-On-A-Stick

Yield: 4 servings

Serve as a vegetable side dish. These can easily be smoked with other foods.

2	yellow squash	¼	cup vegetable oil
2	zucchini	½	teaspoon Italian
2	green peppers, seeded, cut in squares		Herb Seasoning
		1	teaspoon parsley
12	boiling onions (small)		Salt and pepper

Scrub and trim ends of yellow squash and zucchini. Slice all squash in 2-inch rounds. Peel onions and leave whole. Place all in a bowl. Mix oil, seasonings, parsley, salt and pepper to taste. Pour oil mixture over vegetables and gently turn, coating the slices. Spear vegetables on four 10-inch skewers, dividing equally. Place on smoker grid and cook until tender, but still crisp.

Charcoal: Use 3 pounds charcoal, 2 quarts hot water, 1 wood stick and smoke about 45 minutes.
Electric: Use 2 quarts hot water, 1 wood stick and smoke about 45 minutes.
Note: Wood sticks can be eliminated.

Thrifty Barbecued Shish Kabobs

Yield: 8 servings

An inexpensive appetizer or main course. Serve with rice or noodles.

2 cans (12 ounces) luncheon meat	2 green peppers
Kabobs Barbecue Sauce (see recipe)	1 can (1 pound) pineapple chunks, drained (save juice)

Cut luncheon meat into 16 chunks. Marinate chunks in Kabobs Barbecue Sauce for 3 hours. Remove stems and seeds from green peppers and cut into 1-inch squares. Alternate meat, green peppers and pineapple on 8 skewers. Brush with sauce and place on smoker grid. Brush again with sauce before serving.

Charcoal: Use 3 pounds charcoal, 2 quarts hot water, 1 wood stick and smoke 45 minutes to 1 hour.
Electric: Use 2 quarts hot water, 1 wood sticks and smoke 45 minutes to 1 hour.

Kabobs Barbecue Sauce

Yield: ¾ cup

Use this sauce on Thrifty Barbecue Shish Kabobs or ham and beef kabobs.

¼ teaspoon Tabasco	1 tablespoon catsup
¼ cup molasses	¼ cup pineapple juice
¼ cup vinegar	(reserved from
¼ cup oil	Thrifty Kabobs)
½ teaspoon dry mustard	

Combine all ingredients in a jar and shake well before using. Store in refrigerator. Brush on kabobs before smoking. Serve with kabobs.

Sauces, Seasonings and Marinades

Use your favorite flavorings for an extraordinary addition to smoked foods. Super Smoking Sauce, Teriyaki Marinade, Small Game Sauce, Cucumber Marinade or Cajun Barbecue Salt might add the right accent of flavor.

Super Smoking Sauce

Enough sauce for 16 chickens or 2 turkeys. It is equally good when used to smoke any kind of beef, ham, or lamb.

1	pound corn oil margarine	2	tablespoons soy sauce
⅔	cup sherry or red wine	2	cloves garlic, finely chopped
2	tablespoons Worcestershire sauce	½	cup chopped parsley
		2	teaspoon salt
		1	cup water

Combine all ingredients in heavy saucepan and bring to a boil. Lower heat and simmer for 30 minutes. Paint on meat surfaces before, once during and at the end of smoking. Keeps indefinitely refrigerated.

Bordelaise Sauce

Serve with beef.

1	cup red wine	¼	cup finely chopped carrots
¼	cup finely chopped ham	1	can brown gravy

Pour wine in a saucepan and boil down to ⅓ cup. Add other ingredients and simmer over low heat for about 30 minutes.

St. Martinville Tartar Sauce

Naturally a delicious sauce for fish.

4	tablespoons sour pickles	2	cups mayonnaise
4	tablespoons chopped parsley or 3 tablespoons dry parsley	4	green onions, chopped
		2	tablespoons capers
		1	teaspoon dry mustard

Slice pickles, place between paper towels and squeeze juice out; then chop. Stir all ingredients together. Keeps approximately 2 weeks in refrigerator.

Sauces, Seasonings and Marinades

Jezebel Sauce

A delicious condiment with all meats.

1 jar (18 ounces) pineapple preserves	1 jar (5 ounces) horseradish
1 jar (18 ounces) apple jelly	1 tablespoon cracked pepper
1 can (1½ ounces) dry mustard	

Combine all ingredients, blend well. Pour in jelly jars and refrigerate. This will keep indefinitely in refrigerator.

Basic Barbecue Sauce

Yield: a little more than 1 cup

1 cup thick, commercial spaghetti sauce	3 tablespoons brown sugar
3 tablespoons vinegar	1½ teaspoons prepared mustard

Combine all ingredients and simmer for 2 minutes. Very good on beef, pork or fowl.

Lemon Barbecue Sauce

Yield: About 2 cups

¼ cup lemon juice	½ teaspoon chili powder
1 small onion, chopped	½ cup water
1 tablespoon vinegar	½ cup catsup
1 tablespoon Worcestershire sauce	½ teaspoon salt

Mix all ingredients together in a saucepan. Cover and cook slowly for about 15 minutes.

Blue Cheese Steak Sauce

For broiled steaks.

¼	pound butter	2	tablespoons chives
¼	pound blue cheese		or chopped shallots

Blend all ingredients together over low heat, do not boil. Cover a broiled steak with freshly ground pepper and spoon lots of the sauce over the steak.

Yogurt-Dill Sauce

Yield: 1 cup

½	cup mayonnaise	3	scallions, chopped
½	cup yogurt		Salt and pepper
2	tablespoons fresh dill	1	tablespoon capers (optional)

Mix all but the last optional ingredient, adding salt and pepper to taste. If you like, sprinkle capers over top. Good with fish or beef roast.

Chutney Sauce

Yield: 1½ cups

1	cup chutney	1	tablespoon
½	cup catsup		Worcestershire
½	teaspoon lemon juice		sauce

Combine ingredients in a saucepan and heat until well blended. Cool and use on pork or lamb chops.

Bourbon Glaze For Ham

1	cup bourbon	¼	teaspoon ground
1	cup brown sugar, firmly packed		cloves
		1	teaspoon orange peel

Combine all ingredients, stirring until sugar is dissolved. About 1 hour before ham is done, spread half the glaze over ham. Serve remaining glaze with ham.

Rockefeller Sauce

2	packages (10 ounces) frozen, chopped spinach, thawed and thoroughly drained	½	cup bread crumbs
4-5	green onions with tops, finely chopped	2	dashes red hot sauce
1	rib celery, finely chopped	1	tablespoon Worcestershire sauce
Small bunch parsley, finely chopped		2	tablespoons lemon juice
12-15	leaves of lettuce, preferably romaine, chopped	1	ounce Pernod (or Annisette liqueur)
¼	cup mint, finely chopped (optional)	1	tablespoon anchovy paste
2	sticks butter, melted	1½	ounces clam juice (or fresh oyster juice)
		Freshly grated Parmesan cheese	

Combine all ingredients, except cheese, and mix well. All the chopping may be done in a food processor or blender. Sauce can be stored in a covered jar in the refrigerator for later use.

USES:

Grilled oysters on the half shell. Cover oysters with sauce, sprinkle with Parmesan cheese, place on smoker grid or grill and cook until oysters begin curling around the edges.

Grilled tomatoes. Place halved tomatoes in aluminum pie pan, cover with sauce and sprinkle with Parmesan cheese. Place pan on grill or smoker grid and cook in same manner as oysters.

Canned oysters. Canned oysters may be combined with sauce, sprinkled with Parmesan cheese and cooked in a casserole dish on grid of smoker for about 1 hour.

Jack's Mustard Supreme

1	cup dry mustard	2	cups sugar
1	cup white vinegar	2	eggs

Mix mustard and vinegar and let marinate 8 hours. In top section of large double boiler, mix well the sugar and eggs. Add mustard-vinegar marinade. Using a candy thermometer, cook until 210°, stirring occasionally. Refrigerate. This super-mustard will keep for several months under refrigeration. Use care if making in smaller quantities, as there is a tendency to burn.

Horseradish Sauce

Yield: 1¾ cups

1½ cups sour cream	2-3 tablespoons prepared
3 tablespoons fresh	horseradish
chives, snipped	½ teaspoon seasoned salt
¼ teaspoon salt	1 tablespoon lemon juice

Mix all ingredients well and refrigerate for at least 2 hours before using.

Salsa

Yield: About 1 pint

3 large tomatoes, peeled	4 green chiles,
seeded and chopped	chopped
1 onion, finely chopped	½ teaspoon monosodium
1 teaspoon garlic salt	glutamate

Mix all ingredients and allow to marinate at least 30 minutes. Salsa keeps up to one week when refrigerated or can be frozen. Serve Salsa on steaks, hamburgers, eggs or on salad.

Small-Game Sauce

Enough for 3 to 4 pounds of meat.

1 can (16 ounce) tomato	4 strips bacon, diced
purée	2 large onions, diced
½ cup catsup	1 tablespoon brown sugar
2 cups water	2 tablespoons prepared
4 tablespoons vinegar	mustard
1 teaspoon Worcestershire	Seasoned pepper
sauce	

Combine all ingredients in a saucepan and bring to a boil. Reduce heat and simmer until sauce thickens, stirring occasionally. Cool. Brush game with sauce before and after cooking. Serve sauce with game.

Cucumber Mayonnaise

1 cup mayonnaise or ½ cup mayonnaise and ½ cup sour cream	¼ teaspoon curry powder (optional)
3 tablespoons lemon juice Dash of Tabasco	½ cup finely chopped cucumber

Combine all ingredients except cucumber. Drain cucumber well and combine with mayonnaise mixture. Chill for several hours before serving. Very good with smoked salmon.

Sweet-Sour Sauce
For Ham or Pork

Yield: About 2 cups

1 cup sugar	1 cup catsup
1 cup white vinegar	1 cup water

Mix together in a saucepan. Cook over low heat until thick and bubbly, about 1 hour. (Thickens more when cool). Keeps indefinitely in refrigerator. Spread on last 1 hour of smoking.

Chicken-Apricot Sauce

Makes enough for 4 broiler chickens, quartered.

1 jar (8 ounces) apricot preserves	1 bottle Russian salad dressing
1 package dry onion soup mix	

Mix all ingredients and store in jar. This sauce is to be poured over chicken before smoking.

Oriental Marinade

Excellent for ducks.

½   cup soy sauce
½   cup sherry
½   cup oil
1   onion, minced
Dash salt

1   tablespoon grated fresh
    ginger root
1   tablespoon grated
    orange rind

Combine all ingredients. Marinate 2 ducks, cut into pieces, in mixture for 8-12 hours.

Marinade for Smoker Chicken

Yield: Enough sauce for 4 chickens

2   cups (1 pound) butter
    or margarine, melted
Juice of 3 lemons
½   teaspoon each of
    thyme, basil, chili
    powder, oregano, dry
    mustard, salt and cloves

1   tablespoon Worcestershire
    sauce
1   tablespoon tarragon
    vinegar
1   tablespoon sugar
2   cloves garlic, minced

Combine all above ingredients. Marinate chicken in sauce 24 hours. Baste chicken with marinade before smoking and at the end of cooking.

Teriyaki Marinade

May be used on chicken, beef or pork.

½   inch slice ginger
    root
1   clove garlic
½   cup soy sauce
1   tablespoon sugar

1   tablespoon vinegar
1   tablespoon sherry
Monosodium glutamate
    (optional)

Break or cut ginger into 3 or 4 pieces; drop into blender with garlic. Blend for a few seconds and add remaining ingredients. Blend until ginger and garlic are very fine. Overuse of MSG may jade taste buds.

Venison Marinade and Sauce

Good for chicken, steak and hamburgers, too.

¾	cup chopped onion	3	tablespoons Worcestershire sauce
½	cup vegetable oil		
¾	cup water	2	teaspoons salt
⅓	cup lemon juice	½	teaspoon pepper
3	tablespoons sugar		

Sauté onion in oil until tender. Add remaining ingredients. Simmer 15 minutes and cool. Place venison in bowl, pour sauce over meat, and marinate in refrigerator overnight, turning occasionally. Sauce may be kept indefinitely in covered jar in refrigerator, heated, and served with smoked venison.

Cajun Barbecue Salt

	Meat or Poultry		*Seafood*
1	box (26 ounces) of salt	1	teaspoon thyme
1½	ounces black pepper	1	bay leaf crumbled
2	ounces red pepper	1	teaspoon sweet basil
1	ounce garlic powder		
1	ounce chili powder		
1	ounce Monosodium Glutamate		

For seafood add the above to the ingredients for meat and poultry barbecue salt.

Combine the above ingredients and sprinkle over meat, poultry or seafood.

Seasoning Salt

Yield: 1½ cups

1½	cups salt	2	teaspoons garlic salt
2	teaspoons tarragon leaves, crushed	3	tablespoons paprika
		2	teaspoons curry powder
2	teaspoons ground oregano	4	teaspoons dry mustard
		1	teaspoon onion powder

Blend together and pour into containers with shaker tops.

Slimmer Seasoned Salt

Yield: 1 cup

Use to flavor smoked meat, fowl, vegetables and dips.

½ cup salt
2 teaspoons powdered artificial sweetener (concentrated)
½ teaspoon dry mustard
1 teaspoon onion powder
1 teaspoon pumpkin pie spice
1 teaspoon celery seeds, ground

1 teaspoon powdered horseradish
½ teaspoon marjoram or thyme
¼ teaspoon garlic powder
1 tablespoon cornstarch
1 tablespoon paprika
2 tablespoons Monosodium Glutamate (Accent)

In a bowl or jar combine all ingredients and mix thoroughly. Put in an airtight container for storage; need not be refrigerated. Substitute for salt or seasoned salt in recipes. You may cut salt in recipe to ¼ and achieve almost the same results.

Side Dishes

A meal is not complete without the "extras" or Side Dishes. The vegetables, salads, soups, breads and desserts. We have prepared a variety of recipes — some cooked on the water smoker and some cooked with "water pan stock". Select the perfect accompaniment to make the most of your meal.

Venice Stuffed Tomatoes

Yield: 4 servings

4	large, firm, fresh tomatoes	1	tablespoon flour
1	package frozen, chopped spinach, defrosted	½	cup sour cream
3	tablespoons butter or margarine	⅛	teaspoon nutmeg

Salt and pepper
⅓-½ cup bread crumbs
Parmesan cheese

Wash tomatoes and spoon out pulp and seeds. Place tomatoes cut side down to drain off juices and set aside. Drain spinach and squeeze out all liquid, then place in a bowl. Melt 1 tablespoon butter and stir in flour. Add sour cream and seasonings and cook until thickened, stirring constantly. Add spinach to mixture and blend gently. Let cool slightly and fill tomato shells. Top tomatoes with a mixture of bread crumbs and cheese. Put tomatoes in a baking pan or foil pan, uncovered. Place pan with tomatoes on smoker grid and cook about 45 minutes to 1 hour.

Corn in Foil or Husks

Yield: 1 - 2 ears per person

Corn on the cob can be smoke-cooked in the husks or husks removed and wrapped in foil.

	Recipe #1		*Recipe #2*
6	ears of corn with husks	6	ears of corn without husks
1	stick butter or margarine, softened	1	green pepper cut in strips
	Lemon-pepper marinade		Pimentos, chopped
		1	stick butter or margarine
			Salt and pepper

For Recipe #1, pull husks back from corn and remove the silk. Rinse corn and pat dry. Apply generous amounts of butter to each ear of corn and sprinkle with lemon-pepper. Replace the husks and smoke 1½ to 2 hours.

For Recipe #2, remove husks and silk from each ear of corn. Rinse ears and pat dry. Place each ear on a separate piece of foil with strips of green pepper and a few chopped pimentos. Cut butter into pieces and place on top of corn. Season with salt and pepper and wrap securely in foil. Place corn on smoker grid and smoke 1½ to 2 hours.

**Smoked Corn in Foil, Baked Potatoes, Spiced
Acorn Squash, Spiced Acorn Squash with Wild Rice,
Best Ever Baked Beans, Orange Sunshine Carrots**

Best Ever Baked Beans

Yield: 8 - 10 servings

4-5	pounds of canned pork and beans	½	cup molasses
½	cup chopped onion	1	teaspoon Worcestershire sauce
½	cup chopped celery	3-4	drops Tabasco sauce
⅓	cup chopped bell pepper	½	cup barbecue sauce
2	tablespoons prepared mustard	½	cup catsup
		2	strips bacon, uncooked and cut in half

Combine all ingredients, except bacon, in large oven-proof container. Lay bacon strips on top. Place on smoker grid and smoke-cook 2-2½ hours.

Beans and Peppers

Yield: 6 servings

2	cans pork and beans	1	teaspoon dry mustard
½	cup brown sugar	¼	cup chopped green chili peppers
2	tablespoons Worcestershire sauce		

Combine all ingredients and pour into a baking pan or foil pan. Place on either smoker grid and heat uncovered 1-2 hours.

Potato and Onion Casserole

Yield: 4 - 6 servings

4	large potatoes	½	cup milk
3	onions	1½	sticks butter or margarine
1	can cream of celery soup		Salt
1	can cream of mushroom soup		Seasoned pepper

Pare potatoes, soak in cold water 30 minutes. Cut in thin slices. Peel onions and slice thin, separating into rings. Mix soups and milk. In a buttered 3-quart casserole, place layer of potatoes, layer of onion rings and then half of the butter (cut in chunks) and seasonings. Spoon half of the soup mixture over the onions. Repeat layering. Place casserole on smoker grid and smoke 2-3 hours.

Orange Sunshine Carrots

Yield: 6 servings

1	pound carrots	¼	cup brown sugar
½	teaspoon salt	2	oranges

Pare 1 pound carrots and cut into ½-inch slices. Place on a double thickness of heavy-duty foil, sprinkle with salt and brown sugar. Peel oranges, cut into bite size pieces and add to carrots. Seal foil tightly and place on smoker grid. Cook for 2 hours.

Spiced Acorn Squash

Yield: 8 servings

4	medium acorn squash	½	teaspoon ground cloves
½	cup brown sugar	½	teaspoon salt
1	teaspoon cinnamon	½	cup butter
½	teaspoon nutmeg	8	tablespoons orange juice

Wash and cut each squash in half. With a spoon, scrape out the seeds and fibers. Mix together the brown sugar, cinnamon, nutmeg, cloves, salt and butter. Spoon the spice mixture into each squash half and add 1 tablespoon orange juice to each. Place squash on double thickness of foil and place on smoker grid. Smoke-cook for 2-3 hours.

Stuffed Acorn Squash

Yield: 4 servings

2	large acorn squash	2	tablespoons finely chopped water chestnuts
Salt			
1	pound ground lean pork	2	tablespoons minced green onion
½	cup bread or cracker crumbs	2	tablespoons soy sauce

Cut off ¼ of the squash at the stem end to form a cover. Spoon out seeds and fibers. Sprinkle cavity with salt. Combine remaining ingredients for filling. Fill squash with filling and top with stem end. Place squash, cut side up, on a double thickness of heavy-duty foil. Place squash on smoker grid and water-smoke 3-4 hours or until pork filling is completely cooked.

Green Beans Supreme

Yield: 8 servings

2	cans whole green beans		Seasoned pepper
1	can (4 ounces) whole button mushrooms	1	teaspoon soy sauce
1	can cream of mushroom soup	½	teaspoon red pepper flakes
⅓	cup milk	1	ounce dry vermouth
4	ounces sour cream	½	teaspoon onion salt
2	tablespoons mayonnaise	¼	cup slivered almonds
		⅓	cup bread crumbs
			Paprika

Drain and rinse beans, mix with drained mushrooms. In a bowl, mix remaining ingredients, except almonds, bread crumbs and paprika. In a 2-quart casserole or foil pan, place beans and mushrooms. Spoon soup mixture over top and mix slightly. Sprinkle almonds, then bread crumbs, then paprika. Place casserole or foil pan, uncovered, on smoker grid and smoke about 2 hours.

Swiss Baked Potatoes

Yield: 4 servings

3-4	large potatoes	1½	cups grated swiss cheese
	Salt and pepper	½	stick butter or margarine, melted
	Paprika		
1	onion		

Scrub potatoes well and slice very thin, with skins on. Slice onion very thin also. Place a layer of potatoes on a greased double thickness of heavy-duty foil or in a greased foil pan. Sprinkle lightly with salt, pepper and paprika. Add a layer of onions and Swiss cheese. Continue layering, pour melted butter over all and sprinkle with seasoning again. Seal foil or cover foil pan, place on smoker grid and smoke-cook 2-2½ hours.

George's Rice

Yield: 6 servings

½	cup margarine	2	small bay leaves
1	cup chopped celery, with leaves	1	teaspoon chopped parsley
3-4	green onions, chopped	½	teaspoon Beau Monde
1	heaping cup uncooked rice	½	teaspoon tarragon
1	can bouillon	½	teaspoon chervil
1	can (4 ounces) mushrooms with juice		

Cook celery and onions in margarine until soft, then add rice. Put mixture in a 2-quart casserole dish or foil pan. Pour in bouillon, add mushrooms, bay leaves, parsley, Bau Monde, tarragon and chervil. Mix well and cover dish or pan with foil. Place dish on smoker grid and cook 2-3 hours. Stir before serving.

Rice and Broccoli

Yield: 6 servings

1	cup cooked rice	½	teaspoon dry mustard
1	package frozen chopped broccoli, cooked and drained	1	teaspoon seasoned pepper
½	cup chopped celery	1	can cream of chicken soup
½	cup chopped onion	½	soup can of milk
2	tablespoons butter or margarine	8	ounces Velveeta cheese, grated
1	teaspoon Worcestershire sauce	1	can French-fried onion rings
3-4	drops Tabasco sauce		

Sauté celery and onion in butter. To celery and butter add: Worcestershire, Tabasco, dry mustard and seasoned pepper. Then add soup, milk, rice and broccoli. Mix all ingredients well. Add cheese and mix again. Put in greased 2-quart casserole, garnishing with canned French-fried onion rings, if desired. Smoke 1-2 hours.

Green Rice

Yields: 8 - 10 servings

4	cups cooked rice	1	teaspoon Tabasco
1	bunch green onions with tops, chopped		sauce
		1	teaspoon salt
1	whole green pepper, chopped		Seasoned pepper
		2	cups grated
1	cup chopped parsley		cheddar cheese
3	eggs		Bread crumbs
1	cup milk		Parmesan cheese
⅓	cup oil		Paprika
1	tablespoon Worcestershire sauce		

Toss together cooked rice and chopped vegetables. Beat eggs, add milk, oil and seasonings. In a 3-quart buttered casserole or foil pan, combine rice, egg mixture and the cheddar cheese. Top with bread crumbs, Parmesan cheese, then sprinkle with paprika. Cook in smoker, covered, 1-hour and 45 minutes. Uncover and cook for 15 minutes longer.

Apple Salad

Yield: 8 servings

This salad can be made ahead, refrigerated and served at the cookout.

1	cup mayonnaise	2	cups thinly sliced
1	teaspoon Dijon mustard		celery
		¾	cup raisins
4	tablespoons lemon juice	¾	cup chopped walnuts or pecans
4	cups diced unpeeled red Rome apples		Lettuce

Gradually beat (using a whisk) the mustard into the mayonnaise to blend well. Add remaining ingredients, except the nuts and lettuce, mixing well. Cover and chill. Serve on lettuce in large bowl and sprinkle with nuts.

Turkey Summer Salad

Yield: 4 servings

Leftover smoked turkey or chicken is delicious in salads.

2 cups smoked turkey, cut into bite-size pieces	¾ cup mayonnaise
3 tablespoons lemon juice	*Garnishes:*
	Crumbled blue cheese
	Grated hard boiled eggs
1½ cups sliced celery	Salted pecans
Salt and seasoned pepper	Chopped apples

Toss turkey with lemon juice. Let stand in refrigerator 2-3 hours. Add remainder of ingredients and mix well. Chill. Serve in lettuce cups with bowls of garnishes.

Roasted Onions

Yield: 4 servings

4 large white or Spanish onions	½ teaspoon salt
½ cup melted butter or margarine	⅛ teaspoon pepper
	Beef bouillon granules

Clean and core white onions. Baste outsides with butter and fill core with seasoning, beef granules and butter. Wrap onions in foil, leaving top open, and place on smoker grid. Smoke about 45 minutes to 1 hour.

Rice and Artichoke Salad

Yield: 8 servings

1 package Chicken Rice-a-Roni	¼ teaspoon curry
1 jar (6 ounces) marinated artichoke hearts	4-6 green onions, chopped with tops
⅓ cup mayonnaise	¼ cup sliced, stuffed, green olives

Cook Rice-a-Roni according to package instructions. Drain artichokes, reserving the liquid. Cut artichokes in fourths and add to rice. Mix mayonnaise, curry, green onions and olives with the artichoke juice and add all to rice mixture. Gently mix all ingredients well and refrigerate until served.

Crudite Salad

Yield: 4 - 6 servings

This is a great buffet salad that pairs perfectly with Cook'n Ca'jun smoked fowl or game.

6	stalks fresh asparagus or green beans	1	small cucumber, sliced thin
½	cup raw cauliflower flowerettes	¼	cup sliced green onions
½	cup sliced celery		A few sliced radishes
1	small zucchini, sliced thin		or cherry tomatoes
½	cup fresh Brussels sprouts, cut in half		Sherry French dressing or French dressing
½	cup sliced raw mushrooms		Chopped parsley

Cut asparagus on the diagonal, put in a large strainer. Add cauliflower, celery, zucchini and Brussels sprouts. Pour boiling water over all; drain and cool. Toss with the mushrooms, cucumbers, green onions and radishes. Pour dressing over these vegetables and refrigerate for at least 1 hour. Drain off dressing. Serve on chilled salad plates and decorate with chopped parsley.

Five-Layer Salad

Yield: 10 servings

Make this one the day before so the flavors will blend.

1	can cut green beans	1	cup vinegar
1	can petit pois peas	½	cup water
1	can bean sprouts	1	teaspoon basil
1	cup diced celery	1	teaspoon garlic powder
1	cup diced onion	1	teaspoon oregano
1	tablespoon salt		Pimentoes (optional)
1	cup sugar		

Drain first 4 ingredients and layer in order given. Top with a layer of onions. Combine the remaining ingredients in a blender and mix well. Pour dressing over layers and garnish with pimentoes if desired. Cover tightly and refrigerate 24-48 hours. Drain, toss and serve.

Cream of Corn Soup

Remember to save the "water pan stock" when you cook chicken.

2	cups "water pan chicken stock"	2	tablespoons butter or margarine
1	can (17 ounces) cream style corn	2	tablespoons flour
½	cup chopped celery with tops	2	cups half and half cream
2	tablespoons chopped onion		Salt and pepper
			Chopped parsley
			Crumbled crisp bacon

Save the "water pan stock" from smoking chickens. Refrigerate the stock (2-3 cups), then remove excess fat. Simmer "water pan chicken stock", corn, celery and onions for 25 minutes. Put in blender and purée in order for texture to be as smooth as possible. Melt butter, add flour and cook for a few minutes but do not brown. Add cream slowly to butter and flour stirring constantly. Add corn mixture, mix well and season to taste. The flavor is improved by refrigerating overnight. Heat and serve sprinkled with the chopped parsley and crumbled bacon.

French Onion Soup

Another great use of "water pan stock".

5	medium yellow onions	3	tablespoons flour
3	tablespoons butter	6	cups "water pan stock" (beef or chicken)
1	tablespoon oil	½	cup vermouth (optional)
1	teaspoon salt		French bread
¼	teaspoon sugar		Parmesan cheese

Save "water pan stock" from smoking beef or chicken. Refrigerate stock, then remove most of fat when it has chilled. In a large saucepan, melt butter and stir in oil. Add onions and cook, covered, very slowly. Cook for 15 minutes, stirring occasionally. Add salt and sugar (to aid browning). Uncover, increase heat to medium and cook about 45 minutes or until golden brown, stirring often. Add flour and cook a few minutes. In separate saucepan, heat "water pan stock" to boiling and turn off heat, then add to onions. Add vermouth and season to taste. Simmer, covered, for 30-45 minutes. Serve hot with toasted thick slices of French bread sprinkled with Parmesan cheese.

Irresistible Garlic Butter Bread

For rolls, French or Italian bread.

1	pound butter	1	tablespoon dried parsley
1	teaspoon garlic powder or 8 cloves garlic, pressed	2	tablespoons Parmesan cheese
1	teaspoon poppy seeds	½	teaspoon chili powder
1	tablespoon caraway seeds	½	teaspoon dry mustard
½	teaspoon celery seeds, and/or ½ teaspoon celery salt	1	teaspoon Italian seasoning
		1	teaspoon Beau Monde
		1	tablespoon paprika
		½	teaspoon Mei Yen (optional)

Allow butter to come to room temperature. Do not melt! Add all ingredients, mixing well. Cover and refrigerate overnight. Remove and bring back to room temperature before spreading. Spread on bread, wrap bread in foil. Place bread on smoker or grill grid. Can be heated in oven also.

Parmesan Cheese Sticks

Oven recipe.

Sliced bread
Butter or margarine
Parmesan cheese

Sesame seeds or
chili powder

Remove crusts from bread and cut each slice into 3 sticks. Roll each stick in butter, then in grated Parmesan cheese mixed with sesame seeds or chili powder. Arrange sticks, not touching, on a cookie sheet and bake in a preheated oven at 350° for 10-15 minutes.

Onion Bread

1	loaf French bread	1	can (3½ ounces) French fried onion rings
3-4	tablespoons butter or margarine, softened		

Slice bread in half, lengthwise. Spread softened butter on each half. Sprinkle onions on lower half of bread and replace top. Wrap bread in heavy-duty foil and place on smoker grid. Heat for 30-45 minutes or until thoroughly hot.

Tomato-Cheese Bread

1	large or 2 small loaves French bread	½	cup catsup
¼	cup butter or margarine, softened	⅓	cup finely chopped green pepper
1	cup cheddar or Swiss cheese, grated	⅓	cup finely chopped onion
		⅓	cup chopped ripe olives

Cut bread loaf in half, lengthwise. Combine remaining ingredients and spread on each bread half. Put loaf together and wrap in heavy-duty foil. Place bread on smoker grid and heat for 45 minutes or until heated thoroughly.

Herb Rye Bread

1	loaf dark rye bread, sliced	¼	teaspoon pepper
½	cup butter or margarine, softened	¼	teaspoon dry mustard
		¼	teaspoon rosemary
3	tablespoons minced parsley	¼	teaspoon sage
		¼	teaspoon tarragon
1	clove garlic, minced	¼	teaspoon thyme
		½	teaspoon salt

Remove bread from wrapper and set aside. Combine remaining ingredients mixing well. Spread mixture on every other slice of bread. Wrap bread in heavy-duty foil and place on smoker grid. Heat 30 to 45 minutes or until thoroughly hot.

Sunshine Bread

1	loaf unsliced French bread	¼	pound butter or margarine, softened
2	tablespoons prepared mustard	¼	teaspoon celery salt
			American cheese slices

Cut bread loaf into 1-inch diagonal slices almost to the bottom. Combine mustard, butter, celery salt and spread on each slice. Place one slice of cheese between each slice. Wrap bread tightly in heavy-duty foil, place on smoker grid and heat for 30-45 minutes or until cheese has melted.

Flaky Sesame Seed Rolls

Oven recipe.

1	can (8 ounces) refrigerated biscuits	½	cup sesame seeds
		1	stick butter, melted

Divide each biscuit in half. Dip both sides of each half into sesame seeds. Place, touching, in a single layer in a Pyrex 10 X 11-inch baking dish. Pour melted butter overall. Bake in a 400° oven for 10 minutes or until brown. Cool for a few minutes until butter is absorbed. Serve in bread basket, great with outdoor cooking.

Walnut and Pineapple Upside-Down Cake

Yield: 1 layer cake

Bake a cake on the smoker. Using no water or wood sticks, this cake can be baked outside on the smoker.

½	stick butter or margarine	¼	cup sugar
½	cup brown sugar	1	3-ounce package cream cheese, softened
1	small can pineapple slices, drained	½	box pineapple cake mix (or 1 layer cake mix)
	Marachino cherries	1	egg
½	cup chopped walnuts	⅔	cup milk

Melt butter in 9-inch round cake pan or 8-inch square foil pan. Sprinkle brown sugar over butter and arrange pineapple and cherries over this. Sprinkle walnuts around edges of pan and set aside. Blend sugar and cheese until smooth. Add cake mix, egg and milk. Mix at medium speed for 2 minutes. Pour into pan over topping and place on smoker, uncovered. If using 9-inch pan and the pan is completely full, remove about ½ cup of the cake batter so it will not spill over while cooking. After baking, flip pan over to remove cake.

Electric: No water pan, no wood sticks, preheat smoker 10-15 minutes and bake 1 hour or until cake is firm.
Note: Not recommended for charcoal smoker due to fluctuating heat.

Walnut and Pineapple Upside-Down Cake

Smoker Cobbler

This is a cobbler that can be cooked on the smoker or in the oven.

1	can cherry pie filling	2	teaspoons cinnamon
1	can pineapple pie filling	1	yellow cake mix
2	tablespoons lemon juice	1	teaspoon allspice
		1	teaspoon cinnamon
		1	stick butter or margarine

Pour both pie fillings in a 9 X 13-inch foil roasting pan or baking pan. Stir in lemon juice and 2 teaspoons cinnamon. In a bowl mix cake mix, allspice and 1 teaspoon cinnamon and spread over pie filling mixture. Melt butter and pour over cake mix. Cover pan with foil, place pan on smoker grid and cook 1½-2 hours.

Smoke-Baked Apples

Yield: 4 servings

4 red apples	Raisins
Butter, or margarine, softened	Brown sugar

Wash apples and remove stems. Core from stem end and leave base intact. Set each apple on a sheet of foil. Place about 1 teaspoon butter in bottom of apples, add raisins, then brown sugar. Top with another teaspoon butter. Wrap foil thickly around each apple, leaving top open. Place on smoker grid and cook about 1-1½ hours.

Honey Pears

Yield: 6 servings

6 ripe pears
Pinch of cinnamon
Honey

Wash pears and remove stems. Core from the stem end and leave base intact. Set each pear on a sheet of heavy-duty foil. Put a pinch of cinnamon in each pear and fill the cavity with honey. Wrap foil thickly around each pear, place on smoker grid and cook about 1 hour. Serve warm.

Cook'n Ca'jun Fruit Bake

Yield: 12 servings

Here is a delicious fruit bake that can be cooked outdoors on the water-smoker with other foods.

1	large can cling peach halves	3	bananas
1	large can pineapple slices		Lemon juice and grated lemon peel
1	large can pear halves	⅓	cup butter
	Maraschino cherries with stems	¾	cup brown sugar

Drain fruit, dry well on paper towels. Arrange fruit in a 3-quart casserole or in a foil pan large enough to hold all fruit. Cut bananas in large chunks and sprinkle with lemon juice and peel. Add to other fruit. The lemon peps up the flavor and keeps bananas from turning. Melt butter, add brown sugar and pour over fruit. (Rum or orange-flavored liqueur can be sprinkled over fruit also.) Place fruit on smoker grid and cook for 1 hour. While fruit is still hot and before serving, sprinkle with 2 tablespoons of brandy and flame.

Wine-Spice Fruit

Yield: 8 servings

The perfect partner for any smoked game.

1	can (13 ounces) pear halves	1	teaspoon allspice
1	can (13 ounces) peach halves	2	bay leaves
1	stick cinnamon or 1 teaspoon ground cinnamon	½	cup Chablis wine

Pour syrup from pears and peaches into a saucepan. Add cinnamon and allspice, boil rapidly until reduced to 1 cup, adding bay leaves after syrup has simmered 10 minutes. When syrup measures 1 cup, remove from flame and add wine. Pour syrup over drained fruit and chill for several hours or overnight before serving.

Heavenly Hash Cake

2	sticks butter or margarine		*Icing:*
4	tablespoons cocoa	1	large package of large marshmallows, halved
4	eggs	6	tablespoons butter or margarine
2	cups sugar		
1½	cups flour	¾	cup evaporated milk
⅛	teaspoon salt	6	cups (1½ one-pound box) confectioners sugar
2	cups pecans, broken in pieces		
2	teaspoons vanilla	¾	cup cocoa
		3	teaspoons vanilla

For cake, melt butter and cocoa in a medium saucepan over low heat. Meantime, beat eggs with electric mixer adding sugar slowly. Pour butter-cocoa mixture into egg-sugar mixture. Add flour, salt, nuts and vanilla. Pour into grased 9 X 13-inch pan. Bake 30 minutes in a 350° oven. While cake is baking, cut marshmallows in half. Sift sugar and cocoa; melt butter in saucepan and add milk, cooking over low heat. When baked, immediately remove cake to cooling rack. Place marshmallows, cut side down, as thickly as possible on top of cake. Heat milk-butter to boiling, remove from heat, add sugar, cocoa and vanilla. Beat until smooth and pour over cake. Keep refrigerated until served. To serve, cut into 1½-inch squares.

Apple-O-Cake

2½	cups sifted flour	3	eggs
1½	teaspoon pumpkin pie spice	2	cups peeled, grated apples
1	teaspoon baking powder	1	teaspoon vanilla
1	teaspoon soda	½	cup milk
1	teaspoon salt	1	cup seedless raisins
½	cup shortening	1	cup chopped walnuts or pecans
1¾	cups sugar		

Sift together first 5 ingredients. Cream together shortening and sugar. Add eggs one at a time, beating well after each addition. Stir in apples and vanilla. Beginning and ending with dry ingredients, add sifted dry ingredients to creamed mixture alternately with milk. Fold in raisins and nuts. Pour into greased and floured bundt or 10-inch tube pan. Bake in a 350° oven for 45 minutes. Remove from oven and let cool 10 minutes. Remove from pan and finish cooling on wire rack.

Coconut Cream Cake

This is very rich and delicious. It must be kept refrigerated but is great for those hot summer evenings outdoors.

1	box yellow cake mix with pudding	1	can (16 ounces) crushed pineapple, undrained
1	can (16 ounces) sweetened condensed milk	1	carton (16 ounces) whipped topping
1	can (15½ ounces) cream of coconut	1	package (12 ounces) frozen coconut

Bake cake mix according to directions for sheet cake. When cake is done, poke holes into cake with a knife. Mix condensed milk with cream of coconut. Spread mixture over hot cake. Spoon crushed pineapple with juice over cake. Spread whipped topping over pineapple. Sprinkle coconut on top. Best when made the day before and kept refrigerated.

Nut Tartlets

Yield: Makes 24 tartlets

	Crust:		
3	ounces cream cheese	1	tablespoon butter, softened
½	cup butter		
1	cup flour	1	teaspoon vanilla
	Filling:	⅛	teaspoon salt
1	egg	1	cup broken pecan pieces
¾	cup brown sugar		

Crust: Let cheese and butter soften at room temperature. Cream cheese and butter, stir in flour. Chill about one hour. Shape in 2 dozen 1-inch balls. Place in 1¾-inch ungreased muffin tins. Press dough against bottom and sides of cups, bringing the dough above the level of the cups.

Filling: In medium bowl, beat eggs, sugar, butter, vanilla and salt until smooth. Divide one-half pecan pieces and add to filling. Put mixture into muffin cups, top with remaining pecans. Bake at 325° for 25 minutes or until filling is set. Cool and remove from pans.

Potato Chip Cookies

Yield: 3 - 4 dozen

1	cup butter or margarine	
1	cup sugar	
1	egg	
1	teaspoon vanilla	

1½ cups flour
1 cup coarsely crushed potato chips
¾ cup chopped pecans

Cream butter and sugar thoroughly. Blend in egg and vanilla. Stir in flour and mix well. Add potato chips and nuts and refrigerate until dough is firm. Drop by spoonfuls onto greased cookie sheet and bake at 350° for 10 to 12 minutes.

Chewy Squares

1 box brown sugar
2 cups butter or margarine

1½ cups sifted flour
1 teaspoon vanilla

Melt butter and brown sugar in a double boiler. Stir in flour and add vanilla. Pour into a greased 9 X 13-inch pan and bake for 30-40 minutes at 350°. Cut into 1½-inch squares.

Sugar Plum Cake

2 cups sugar
1 cup oil
3 eggs
2 jars (4¾ ounces) baby food plums with tapioca

1 teaspoon cinnamon
1 teaspoon cloves
2 cups self-rising flour

Blend together all ingredients in the order listed. Pour into a greased and sugared bundt cake pan or 10-inch tube pan. Bake at 350° for 45 minutes to 1 hour. Remove from oven and let cake cool 10 minutes in pan before turning out.

Glaze

¾ cup plum jam or jelly
1 teaspoon lemon juice

For glaze, simply heat plum jam and lemon juice. Add a little water if glaze is too thick. Pour over cake while warm.

Grill

It's so nice to have a water smoker that easily converts to a grill. Enjoy your smoker-grill with recipes such as Marinated Steak, Whiskey Chicken, Broiled Leg of Lamb, Marinated Shrimp, Cheddar Bread or Grilled Banana Shortcake. Don't forget the American favorite — Burgers, Burgers with Mushrooms, Reuben Burgers, Taco Burgers, Near East Burgers and "Ham" Spiced Burgers are a few of the gourmet burger specialties we hope you enjoy.

Basic Grilled Hamburgers

For maximum flavor and adequate fat content, we recommend using a high grade of beef with between 15 and 20 percent fat content. If the fat content is higher you will have constant flare-ups and if it is lower the grilled meat will tend to be dry. Mix all the ingredients together quickly and do not overhandle. The less it is handled the more tender and juicy the burgers will be. Burgers made of cooked meats, poultry, fish or vegetables require less cooking time.

To grill, convert Cook'n Ca'jun for grilling. *For charcoal:* Grill is ready when coals are covered with ash and glowing in center. *For electric and gas:* Preheat for 10-15 minutes or until unit is hot. Place greased grid in place and arrange patties on grid. Grill-cook burgers 5-10 minutes on each side, depending on degree of doneness desired, thickness of patties and recipe variations. For protection from heat, use protective mitts and long-handled utensils.

Quick Tomato-Onion Burgers

Yield: 6 servings

1½	pounds ground beef	¼	cup water
1	envelope tomato-onion soup mix	1	teaspoon salt
		½	teaspoon pepper

Combine all ingredients and form into 6 patties. Place patties on grill grid and cook 5-10 minutes on each side. Serve with onion rolls or hamburger buns.

Tex-Mex Burgers

Yield: 6 - 8 servings

1½	pounds ground beef	3	tablespoons evaporated milk
1	can (8 ounces) jalapeno bean dip	1	teaspoon salt
½	cup cornflake crumbs		Avocado slices

Combine all ingredients, except avocado slices, and shape into 6-8 patties. Grill patties about 5-10 minutes on each side and serve topped with sliced avocados and toasted English muffins.

Grilled Burgers

Hot Dog Burgers

Yield: 4 - 6 servings

1½	pounds ground beef	¼	teaspoon salt
⅓	cup crushed potato chips	¼	teaspoon pepper
		6	dill pickle spears
2	tablespoons hot prepared mustard		Hot dog buns
			Chili sauce
			Chopped onions

Combine beef, potato chips, mustard, salt and pepper. Divide mixture into 6 parts and wrap around 6 dill pickle spears. Grill 5-10 minutes on both sides and serve on hot dog buns with chili sauce and chopped onions.

Taco Burgers

Yield: 10 - 12 tacos

1¾	pounds ground beef	1	onion sliced
			Shredded lettuce
2	packages taco seasoning mix		Green chilies, chopped
¼	cup evaporated milk		Tomatoes, chopped
	Taco shells		Cheddar cheese, grated

Combine ground beef, taco seasoning and milk. Shape into half circles to fit taco shells. Grill meat 5-10 minutes on each side and serve in shells with onion, lettuce, chilies, tomatoes and cheese.

Bagel Burgers

Yield: 6 - 8 servings

1½	pounds ground beef	2	tablespoons horseradish
½	cup finely chopped dill pickles	1½	teaspoons salt
		¼	teaspoon pepper
¼	cup chopped scallions		Bagels and cream cheese

Combine all ingredients, except bagels and cream cheese, and form into doughnut shaped patties. Grill for 5-10 minutes on each side and serve on sliced, grilled bagels with cream cheese.

Green Goddess Burgers

Yield: 6 servings

1¾ pounds ground beef	1 package (10 ounces)
2 tablespoons evaporated milk	frozen chopped spinach, cooked and drained
2 teaspoons salt	
¼ teaspoon pepper	1 tablespoon Green
2 hard-cooked eggs, chopped	Goddess salad dressing

Combine beef, milk, salt and pepper. Shape into 12 patties. Combine spinach, eggs and Green Goddess salad dressing. Spread mixture on 6 patties and top with remaining patties; press edges to seal. Grill for 5-10 minutes on both sides. Serve on buns with additional Green Goddess dressing and cherry tomatoes.

Near East Burgers

Yield: 6 servings

2 pounds ground lamb	1 teaspoon ground coriander
¾ cup chopped peanuts	
½ cup soft bread crumbs	½ teaspoon curry powder
½ cup chopped onion	½ teaspoon grated lemon rind
1 egg	
1 teaspoon salt	1 teaspoon pepper

Combine all ingredients and shape mixture into 6 patties. Grill for 5-10 minutes on each side and serve on hamburger buns.

"Ham" Spiced Burgers

Yield: 6 - 8 servings

2 pounds ground cooked ham	2 tablespoons chopped parsley
3 eggs	1 teaspoon lemon juice
2 tablespoons prepared mustard	½ teaspoon cinnamon
	½ teaspoon cloves

Combine all ingredients and shape into 6-8 round patties. Grill 5-10 minutes on each side and serve on waffles, topped with pineapple rings. Perfect for breakfast or brunch dish.

Reuben Burgers

Yield: 6 servings

1	pound ground beef	1	tablespoon caraway
1	can (12 ounces) corned		seeds
	beef, chopped	1	teaspoon salt
1	egg		Swiss cheese, grated
½	cup pumpernickel		Sauerkraut, drained
	bread crumbs		Pumpernickel bread

Combine first 6 ingredients and form into 12 patties. Place 1 tablespoon grated cheese and 1 tablespoon drained sauerkraut on top of 6 patties. Top with other 6 patties and press edges to seal. Grill for 5-10 minutes on each side and serve on pumpernickel bread.

Sausage-Egg Burgers

Yield: 6 servings

¾	pound bulk pork	½	teaspoon thyme
	sausage	½	teaspoon seasoned
¾	pound ground beef		pepper
1	teaspoon salt	6	hard cooked eggs
½	teaspoon sage		

Combine all ingredients, except eggs. Wrap mixture around 6 hard cooked eggs. Grill until well done. Serve sliced in half on hamburger buns with catsup.

Burgers With Mushrooms

Yield: 6 - 8 servings

2	pounds ground	1	can (3 ounces)
	beef		mushrooms, drained
2	eggs		and chopped
2	tablespoons bread	1	teaspoon salt
	crumbs	1	teaspoon seasoned salt
1	medium onion, chopped	1	tablespoon Worcestershire
1	green pepper, chopped		sauce
1	teaspoon pepper		

Shape into 6-8 patties and grill 5-10 minutes on each side. Serve on buns with relishes.

Tuna-Cheese Burgers

Yield: 6 servings

3	cans (6½-7 ounces each) tuna	2	eggs, beaten
¾	cup soft bread crumbs	1	tablespoon chopped capers
¼	cup heavy cream	2	teaspoons dry mustard
¼	cup chopped celery	½	teaspoon onion salt
¼	cup chopped parsley		American cheese slices

Drain tuna and put through fine blade of food grinder or grind in food processor. Combine with remaining ingredients except cheese. Form into 6 patties and chill for 1 hour. Grill on one side and top with American cheese slices after turning. Serve on rolls with sliced tomato and tartar sauce.

Turkey-Cran Burgers

Yield: 6 servings

3	cups cooked, finely chopped turkey	¼	cup heavy cream
¼	cup butter or margarine	½	teaspoon poultry seasoning
2	eggs	½	teaspoon nutmeg
⅔	cup fresh white bread crumbs	½	teaspoon salt
			Swiss cheese slices
			Cranberry sauce

Combine all ingredients except cheese and cranberry sauce. Shape into 6 round patties and chill 1 hour. Grill on each side, adding a slice of Swiss cheese after turning. Top each with round slice of cranberry sauce and serve on toasted sliced bread.

Stroganoff Burgers

Yield: 6 servings

2	pounds ground veal or beef	1	cup chopped mushrooms
⅓	cup heavy cream	2	tablespoons chopped fresh parsley
2	teaspoons salt		
1	teaspoon marjoram	2	tablespoons butter or margarine
1	teaspoon grated lemon peel		Black bread and sour cream
½	teaspoon pepper		

Combine first six ingredients and shape into twelve 4-inch squares. Sauté mushrooms and parsley in butter for a few minutes. Spread mushroom mixture on 6 squares and top with remaining 6 squares. Press edges together to seal. Grill for 5-10 minutes on each side. Serve on black bread, spread with sour cream.

Gourmet Butter for Steak

Broil steaks with a small amount of seasoning and while hot, top with one of these butters.

Butter #1

1	stick butter, softened
1	tablespoon finely chopped chives
1	tablespoon finely chopped parsley
2	teaspoons lemon juice
⅛	teaspoon red pepper

Butter #2

1	stick butter, softened
1	cup canned garbanzo beans, drained and mashed
1	tablespoon prepared mustard

Butter #3

1	stick butter, softened
4	pimento stuffed olives, chopped
1	teaspoon finely chopped parsley
⅛	teaspoon white pepper
	Salt

Butter #4

1	stick butter, softened
2	hard-cooked eggs, sieved
¼-½	teaspoon curry powder

For each butter, combine all ingredients until well blended. On wax paper, form the mixture into a rectangle like a stick of butter. Wrap tightly and secure ends. Refrigerate until butter holds shape; about 30 minutes. To serve, remove wrap, cut into cubes and place on hot steaks to melt.

Steak Au Poivre Vert

Yield: 3 servings

Steak with green peppercorns.

1 3-pound sirloin steak, 1- to 1½-inches thick	1 tablespoon drained, green peppercorns, coarsely crushed
Salt	
1 tablespoon cognac or whisky	¼ cup heavy cream
	½ teaspoon Dijon mustard

Cut off pieces of fat from steaks and reserve. Grease grill grid to avoid sticking. Place steak on grill and cook to desired doneness. Remove from grill and place on warm platter. Season with salt and keep warm. In a skillet melt steak fat and stir in cognac or whiskey while continuing to heat. Add crushed green peppercorns and cream. Bring to a simmer, constantly stirring. Stir in the mustard and pour sauce over steak.

Marinated Steak

Yield: ½ pound per serving

Marinating this steak makes it more tender and tasteful.

1 top round steak or chuck steak, 3-inches thick	½ bottle (4 ounces) concentrated lime juice
Coarse ground pepper	Salt
1 clove garlic, minced	
½ bottle (4 ounces) soy sauce	

Pepper steak and place in marinating dish. Combine garlic, soy sauce and lime juice. Pour over steak. Let stand several hours or overnight in refrigerator, turning occasionally. Remove from marinade and place on grill. Brush with marinade before grilling and seasoning with salt. Cook to desired doneness, about 45 minutes to 1 hour.

Mustard Steak

Yield: 2 servings

Mustard adds a peppy tang to thick broiled steaks.

1	sirloin steak or 2 T-bone steaks, 1½-inches thick	¼	cup prepared mustard
½	cup butter, softened	½	teaspoon celery seeds
			Salt and pepper (optional)

Trim excess fat from steak and score remaining fat. Pat steak dry. Combine butter, mustard, and celery seeds. Spread mustard mixture on both sides of steak. Place steaks on grid for grilling. Grill steaks 4-5 minutes on each side for rare, 5-6 minutes for medium and 6-8 minutes for well-done.

Barbecued Flank Steak

Yield: 4 servings

1	flank steak	1	clove garlic, minced
¼	cup soy sauce	1	teaspoon oregano
1	tablespoon vinegar		Salt and pepper
2	tablespoons oil		

Pound steak to tenderize. Combine remaining ingredients. Place steak in a glass shallow dish and pour soy mixture over steak. Marinate steak for 3-4 hours. Place steak on grill, brush with marinade and grill 3-5 minutes on each side. Carve in thin diagonal slices.

Lemon-Herb Grilled Pork Chops

Yield: 6 servings

Serve with foil-wrapped corn on the cob and a salad.

6	pork chops, ¾-inch thick	1	teaspoon salt
½	cup lemon juice	½	teaspoon each of ground thyme, oregano and seasoned pepper
4	tablespoons oil		
3-4	cloves garlic, minced		

Place pork chops in a glass shallow dish. Combine remaining ingredients to make marinade. Pour over chops, cover and marinate overnight in refrigerator. Remove chops from sauce and reserve marinade for serving. Place chops on grid and grill about 30 minutes or until completely done, brushing with marinade and turning occasionally.

Grilled Ham With Plum Sauce

Yield: 8 - 12 servings

A delicious and pretty ham to serve from the grill.

1	canned ham (7 pounds), cut lengthwise in half or 2 center-cut ham slices, 2- to 3-inches thick	2	tablespoons vinegar
		¼	cup catsup
		½	teaspoon ground ginger
2	jars (10 ounces each) plum jelly or jam	2	tablespoons cornstarch
		¼	cup water
¾	cup water		Parsley

If using canned ham, rinse and prepare for grilling. Trim excess fat on ham. Heat jelly, ¾ cup water, vinegar, catsup and ginger over medium heat, stirring constantly until jelly melts. Mix cornstarch and ¼ cup water; stir into jelly mixture and heat to boiling, stirring constantly. Boil and stir 2 minutes. Place ham on grill. Cook, basting frequently with plum sauce, until meat thermometer registers 140°, about 30 minutes (15 minutes on each side). Arrange ham on platter, garnish with parsley and serve with remaining plum sauce.

Grilled Chicken

Yield: ½ chicken per serving

Quite a dish!

3-4	pounds chicken broilers	2	tablespoons chopped
2	sticks butter or		rosemary
	margarine	½	cup oil
1	·teaspoon pepper	1	teaspoon salt
2	tablespoons chopped	1	lemon
	parsley		

Half each chicken through the breast, rub well with a mixture of 1 stick melted butter seasoned with pepper, parsley and rosemary. While rubbing mixture into chickens, loosen skin around neck and slide hand underneath and rub mixture into flesh.

When you remove whatever you have been smoking on the water-smoker (using 10-15 pounds charcoal) you should have a good hot bed of coals. Place chickens on grid, bone side down and cook 15 to 20 minutes, brushing the up side with a combination of the following: 1 stick melted butter, ½ cup oil, 1 teaspoon salt and juice of 1 lemon. Turn chicken, baste well and grill on flesh side about 15 to 20 minutes, brushing often with basting mixture. Watch to make sure skin does not blister or char. Allow chicken to rest a few minutes before serving with remainder of basting sauce. This recipe can be prepared on gas or electric grill also.

Whisky Chicken

Yield: 4 servings

Using a bottled barbecue cooking sauce with a little whisky gives chicken a remarkable flavor.

1	3- to 4-pound chicken,	½	cup whisky
	cut in serving pieces	1	teaspoon salt
1	bottle (8-10 ounces)	½	teaspoon pepper
	barbecue cooking sauce		
	(non-sweet if available)		

Rinse chicken and pat dry. Place chicken in a large shallow dish. Combine remaining ingredients and pour over chicken. Let chicken stand in sauce in refrigerator 3-4 hours, turning occasionally. Place chicken on grill grid, brush liberally with sauce several times while grilling. Grill 30-45 minutes turning once.

Broiled Boned Leg of Lamb

Yield: 6 servings

Use gin or white wine to enhance the flavor of this leg of lamb.

1 4- to 5-pound leg of lamb, boned not rolled	1 teaspoon white pepper
2 tablespoons rosemary	Gin or white wine
1 teaspoon basil	3 tablespoons butter, melted

Cut leg almost in half and butterfly. Gently pound flat. Sprinkle with salt, rosemary, basil and pepper. Let rest 1 hour to absorb seasoning flavors. Place on grill and cook 10-15 minutes on each side. Baste with gin or wine during last 10 minutes. Remove and let rest 15 minutes on heated platter. Brush on melted butter, slice thin and serve with juices.

Lamb Patties Shaki

Yield: 4 servings

This is a delicious main course or served as burgers.

¼ teaspoon whole saffron	1 teaspoon ground cumin seed
1 tablespoon boiling water	½ teaspoon ground ginger
3 tablespoons instant minced onion	½ teaspoon ground cardamon
⅓ cup water	¼ teaspoon ground black pepper
1 pound ground lean lamb	⅛ teaspoon ground cloves
2 tablespoons flour	2 tablespoons lemon juice
1 egg, lightly beaten	2 tablespoons plain yogurt
1 teaspoon salt	
1 tablespoon ground coriander	

Crumble saffron in boiling water, set aside. Rehydrate minced onion in ⅓ cup water for 10 minutes. In a large mixing bowl combine lamb with flour, egg, salt and spices. Add lemon juice, yogurt, saffron mixture and onion. Mix well but do not overmix. Shape into patties, dip lightly in flour, shaking off excess. Place patties on grill and cook about 15 minutes on each side.

Cajun Cognac Lamb Steak

Yield: 4 - 6 servings

A great recipe for those who love lamb.

6	lamb steaks or shoulder chops, cut 1-inch thick	4	teaspoons dry mustard
¾	cup butter or margarine	1	tablespoon Worcestershire sauce
		½	cup cognac
			Chopped parsley

Broil steaks on grill 4 to 6 minutes on each side, depending on desired degree of doneness. Melt butter in a pan on grill, stir in mustard and Worcestershire sauce. Stir in cognac, heat slightly and ignite. Arrange steaks on platter and pour some of the sauce on meat. Sprinkle with parsley. Serve remaining sauce with steaks.

Grilled Halibut Steaks

Yield: 4 - 6 servings

Fresh or frozen fish can be used.

4	halibut, haddock or turbot steaks (2 lbs.)	2	green onions, finely chopped
⅓	cup oil	½	teaspoon ginger
¼	cup lemon juice	½	teaspoon onion salt
¼	cup soy sauce	¼	teaspoon pepper

Place fish in a large glass dish. Combine remaining ingredients and pour over fish. Cover dish and marinate at room temperature about 1 hour. Remove fish steaks from marinade and place on greased grid. Grill about 15 minutes or until fish flakes easily. Baste with marinade several times while grilling.

Grilled Lobster Tails

Yield: 4 servings

A treat for special occasions.

4 lobster tails, thawed if frozen	1 clove garlic, minced
1 stick butter, melted	¼ cup dry white wine
½ teaspoon paprika	¼ teaspoon salt
1 tablespoon Worcestershire sauce	Dash of pepper

Cut the lobster tails almost through the membrane on underside and spread open. Combine remaining ingredients and spread on lobster flesh. Place lobster on grill, shell side down. Cook about 4-5 minutes, turn and cook an additional 3-4 minutes. Lobster is done when flesh turns milky white. Serve with remaining sauce.

Marinated Shrimp

Yield: 24 appetizers

Always a favorite at any party!

2 pounds medium or large shrimp	3 tablespoons finely chopped parsley
½ cup oil	2 tablespoons finely chopped onion
¼ cup soy sauce	½ teaspoon salt
½ cup lemon juice	¼ teaspoon cayenne pepper
1 small clove garlic, minced	

Shell, devein and place shrimp in a shallow dish. Combine remaining ingredients and pour over shrimp. Cover and let stand in refrigerator 1-2 hours. Remove from marinade. If desired, thread on skewers. Grill for about 5-7 minutes, basting with marinade occasionally.

Pungent Fish Fillets

Yield: 4 - 6 servings

The combination of the milk and Worcestershire sauce produces an extraordinary pungent flavor.

2	pounds fresh or frozen fish fillets	¼	cup Worcestershire sauce
1	cup buttermilk	½	teaspoon garlic powder

Thaw fish if frozen. Place fish in a large glass dish. Combine other ingredients and pour over fish. Let stand in milk mixture about 30 minutes at room temperature. Remove fish from dish and place on greased grid and top with milk mixture. Grill about 15 minutes. Garnish with parsley and serve.

Low Calorie Chicken Livers

Yield: 6 servings

Serves 6 amply with about 120 calories per serving.

1	pound chicken livers	½	teaspoon Italian Herb seasoning
1	cup Diet Italian Salad Dressing		

Rinse livers, put in a shallow bowl and combine with Italian Dressing and Italian Herb mix. Let marinate for 3-4 hours. Thread on skewers and place on grill grid. Broil on grill for about 7-10 minutes and baste with marinade before serving.

Mushroom Tidbits

Fresh large mushrooms	Longhorn cheese
Lemon juice	Pimentos

Wash mushrooms, remove stems and brush with lemon juice. Cut cheese in small squares of appropriate size to fit into mushroom caps. Lay strips of pimento across cheese. Place mushrooms in a foil pan or on heavy-duty foil that has been doubled. Grill for 10-15 minutes or until cheese melts.

Rumaki

Yield: 18 appetizers

This popular appetizer is more tasty when cooked on the grill.

18	chicken livers	1	tablespoon lemon juice
18	water chestnuts		
9	thin bacon strips, halved	¼	teaspoon ginger
		¼	teaspoon curry powder
½	cup soy sauce		

Wrap each liver around a water chestnut. Then wrap each piece of bacon around the chicken liver and water chestnut, securing with a toothpick. Combine remaining ingredients and pour over the rumaki. Marinate at least 1 hour. Place on grill and cook for 6-8 minutes, turning once.

Special Baked Potatoes

Yield: 6 servings

6	medium potatoes	6	onion slices
6	slices cheese	6	slices bacon

Cut thin wedge from center of potato. Place cheese and onion slices in open wedges. Wrap potatoes with bacon slices and wrap each potato in heavy-duty foil. Grill for about 1 hour.

Grill Baked Beans

Yield: 6 - 8 servings

2	cans (1 pound 12 ounces each) pork and beans	2	medium onions, chopped
2	dashes liquid red pepper	2	cups grated cheddar cheese

Combine all ingredients in a 2-quart casserole or foil pan. Place on grill and cook 45 minutes.

Dessert Fruit Kabobs

Yield: 6 servings

Something sweet on a stick.

2	navel oranges, sliced ½-inch thick	2	bananas, cut in 1-inch slices
1	seedless pink grapefruit, sliced ½-inch thick	1	cup brown sugar
		1	cup water
1	small honeydew melon, sliced ½-inch thick, rind removed	½	teaspoon ground cloves
		1	tablespoon butter or margarine
12	unpeeled apple wedges		

Cut orange and grapefruit slices into quarters; cut melon slices into equivalent size wedges. Spear an apple wedge on each of six skewers, then alternate with wedges of grapefruit, bananas, orange and melon; repeat. Set aside. Mix brown sugar, water and cloves in a saucepan. Stir over medium heat and bring to a boil, stirring until clear and thickened. Remove from heat, stir in butter and spoon over fruit kabobs. Place skewers with fruit on grill and cook 5-6 minutes, rotating and basting with syrup. Serve hot as a dessert. Save remaining sauce for dunking.

Peach and Berry Cobbler

Yield: 8 - 10 servings

Delicious! For variety, substitute blueberries, raspberries or strawberries for the blackberries.

2	cups blackberries	½	teaspoon cinnamon
2	cups peaches	¼	teaspoon cloves
1	tablespoon lemon juice	¾	cup flour
		⅓	cup quick cooking oats
½	cup sugar	½	cup brown sugar
¼	cup flour	⅓	cup butter or margarine

Combine first 6 ingredients in a foil pan or 9 X 9 - inch cake pan. In a bowl combine remaining ingredients, cutting in butter as for pie crust. Sprinkle butter mixture over fruit, cover with foil and place on smoker grill. Grill for 45 minutes to 1 hour.

Note: This recipe can also be cooked in the water-smoker for about 1½ — 2 hours.

Grilled Banana Stackcake

Yield: 4 servings

¼ cup butter
3 firm bananas, peeled and quartered
2 tablespoons lemon juice
2 tablespoons orange juice

⅔ cup brown sugar
¼ teaspoon cinnamon
Dash nutmeg
8 slices pound cake, 1-inch thick
Whipped cream

Melt butter in 7 X 11-inch foil pan. Add bananas; drizzle with fruit juices, sprinkle with brown sugar, cinnamon and nutmeg. Cook on grill until bananas are soft. Spoon syrup over bananas occasionally. Toast cake slices on both sides on grill. To serve spoon half bananas and syrup over 4 cake slices; add remaining cake slices and top with remainder of bananas and syrup. Top with whipped cream and serve.

Cheddar Bread

1 loaf French bread, unsliced
½ cup butter or margarine, softened

1 cup grated cheddar cheese
1 teaspoon dill seed
½ clove garlic, crushed

Slice loaf in half, lengthwise. Combine remaining ingredients and spread on one half. Put the bread halves together and wrap in foil. Heat on the grill for about 20 minutes or until cheese has melted.

INDEX

D

Desserts,

E

Electric Cooking Chart

F

Fish and Seafood,

G

Gas Cooking Chart
Grill Recipes,